Magic On Th

by

Tylluan Penry

To Michael
Always believe in magic!
Brightest Blessings
Tylluan Penry

The Wolfenhowle Press

Magic on the Breath

ISBN 978-0-9570442-0-3

Cover Design and Illustrations by Drew Thomas

Published by:

The Wolfenhowle Press
Redcroft,
Nile Road,
Trealaw
Tonypandy
CF40 2UY

http://thewolfenhowlepress.com

Printed by: Book Printing UK, Remus Drive, Coltsfoot Drive, Woodston, Peterborough PE2 9BF

This book is dedicated with love to GMJM - a wonderful daughter and friend.

Other Titles by Tylluan Penry :

Seeking the Green (published by Capall Bann, 2008)

The Magical Properties of Plants - and How to Find Them (published by Capall Bann, 2009)

The Essential Guide to Psychic Self Defence (published by Capall Bann 2010)

Contents

About Tylluan Penry

Tylluan Penry is a solitary pagan witch, independent scholar and the author of books on magic and folklore including *Seeking the Green, The Magical Properties of Plants and how to find them* and *The Essential Guide to Psychic Self Defence*.

Tylluan has been a popular and regular speaker at various events including Witchfest International, The Artemis Gathering, Witchfest England and Witchfest Wales. She has also given talks for the Pagan Federation, and at independent, private events. Her articles have appeared in a variety of publications including *Witchcraft & Wicca* and *Myddle Earth*.

She has her own internet radio show, *The Magical World of Tylluan Penry* at www.oneworldradio.org.uk and is regularly consulted by the media for advice in portraying witchcraft and paganism. Tylluan is well known for her no-nonsense, down-to-earth approach, and is also a skilled, compassionate and experienced rune reader.

Tylluan is married, has a large family, many pets, an overgrown garden and lives in the South Wales Rhondda Valley.

Preface

This book is designed to be a straightforward guide to a simple but powerful magical technique. Everything in these pages is based on my own personal practice and experience through the years.

I wanted to create a book that you, the reader, could begin using straight away, with nothing to distract you from the technique itself. For that reason, unlike my earlier books, *The Magical Properties of Plants and How to Find Them* and *The Essential Guide to Psychic Self Defence, Magic on the Breath* does not contain the usual footnotes or a Bibliography.

If you want to perform magic and cast spells, as opposed to simply thinking and day dreaming, then you have to practise it rather than theorise about it.

Only then will you be the person you were meant to be.

Brightest blessings

Tylluan Penry

Rhondda Valley, Wales,
Samhain, 2011

Chapter One

This is not a book of spells. Rather, it is a book of magical techniques. The two are quite different. A book of spells provides you with a written formula for the various types of magic you might need. Life being what it is, there will always be some situations for which you cannot find a suitable ready-made spell. A book of magical techniques however, teaches you skills, principles of magic and basic techniques. Once you have mastered these you can create your own individual spells for any and every situation.

The underlying principle behind Magic on the Breath is that spells can be empowered by our breathing (especially as we exhale). In fact there is a process of chemical transformation going on – whether we're aware of it or not – every single time we breathe in oxygen from the air around us and then change it into carbon dioxide as we breathe out. The idea that the breath has its own innate power is nothing new. The ancient Greeks referred to it as *dynamis* and even today we often describe powerful energetic people as 'dynamic'.

If we look at this transformation from a magical point of view, it makes perfect sense. When we breathe in we bring the outside world into our body. This is then empowered and transformed by our will or intention, and sent on its way as we breathe out. All we have to do is learn to control and adapt our breathing so that it carries our magical intention to its proper destination. Over many years of teaching magic and spell craft, I have noticed that different spells require slightly different breathing techniques. They are all easy to learn and once you've mastered them they can be adapted for almost any type of spell.

There is no single 'correct' way to cast a spell. Some people like to cast a circle first, perhaps marking the four compass points with salt, water, candles and incense. Others like to follow complicated rituals in strange languages, or swear by exotic ingredients or magical correspondences, trying to match their spell with the correct day of the week or hour of the day, or even with metals, crystals, colours and plants. This is fine if you have the knowledge and the patience for it. But it's not essential and there's certainly no single 'correct' way to perform magic. In fact it's quite possible to cast spells using nothing but our bare hands. But the thing that really makes the magic work is simplicity itself – our belief, our will.

One of the first things you must believe is that magic is possible, and that you can do it. This might seem obvious, but it's surprising how many people try to cast a spell while secretly thinking about other things such as what to cook for tea. If you do this, you simply aren't giving yourself or your magic a proper chance. You get the best results when you have complete faith in your own abilities. Doubt is a self-fulfilling prophecy. If you think you *might* fail, you almost certainly will. And the opposite holds true, too. If you believe in yourself and the techniques you are using you are giving your magic the best possible chance of success.

However, we have to be realistic. Most people don't feel particularly confident, especially in the early days. It isn't easy to persuade yourself to keep trying when you're not getting the results you hoped for. But actually most magical work is simply a matter of aptitude, and you need to find out what sort of spells you're best at. For example, some people are very good at wart charming. They only have to look at the offending growth and it promptly withers and dies. Others, including myself, find wart charming difficult even though when I was a child my hands were covered in them.

Nowadays of course most people would just go straight to the doctors and get them frozen, but in my day, growing up in a family of witches, this was seen as an opportunity for me to learn a new skill. The cryptic suggestions came thick and fast. I remember being told that my great-grandmother would always charm warts away just after a full moon. So I took the hint and duly sat out in the garden under the next full moon, trying to get the warts to disappear. Nothing happened.

Next, an aunt suggested using dandelions at a full moon. Dandelions were large and round, like the moon, she assured me, and they would make the warts vanish. So four weeks after my first attempt, I was back out in the garden, waving a dandelion and muttering at my warts. Again nothing happened. The next full moon, after yet more hints and clues, I tried again, this time piercing the warts with a shiny new pin. But still nothing happened. So I know a little bit about feeling discouraged when magic doesn't seem to work. Yet even though my first efforts were hopeless, what was important was the suggestion that charming warts was possible and that others had done it before me. So I kept on trying, month after month, convinced there had to be a way to rid myself of them.

What I didn't know then of course, is that it is precisely this determination, this will to accomplish something that forms the basis of all successful spells. So while I may not have had much success charming my warts, I was in fact learning a great deal about focussing my will. In the end the weather was getting cold and sitting out under the moon for any length of time was becoming difficult, so my mother suggested selling my warts. And unbelievably, it worked! I 'sold' them (by now I had almost thirty) to a girl who lived nearby and who didn't believe in magic. By the end of the week they had all disappeared.

I have to admit though, that there was a downside to this particular spell. The next time I saw the girl, she was coming out of the chemists with her mother, clutching a bottle of Wart Solvent, her hands covered in sticking plasters. I don't think either of them ever spoke to me again. And to this day, I still don't consider wart charming is one of my strong points!

Getting started – remembering our inner magic
Before we even think about performing magic and sorting out our breathing techniques, we need to try and rediscover our own, unique, inner magic. Sometimes people claim that magic has never played any part in their lives although actually that's very rare. At some point – especially in childhood when we're more receptive to such things - most of us have experienced a moment or two of magic.

So what you need to do now is to think back to such a time. I call them 'magical episodes.' It might have been a day when we felt we had healed someone, or somehow 'knew' something was going to happen, or even had a gut feeling about another person that turned out to be true. You don't need to be able to explain what happened, or how the magic might have worked, but you do need to try and remember what it felt like, that feeling that 'something was going on.' Spend a little time just thinking about the ways magic has turned up in your life. It's probably always been there, in the background, just waiting for you to notice it and give it its due.

For example, young children often report seeing fairies and other magical beings that are invisible to the adults around them. This ability seems to vanish by the time we reach our teens, possibly because by then the child has been repeatedly told that fairies don't exist. Yet the memory of that time when we *did* believe still remains, although you may have to dig deep to find it again.

The most amazing thing about these magical episodes is that they are never completely forgotten. Maybe they were very few and far between, sometimes just a fleeting second or two of recognition. Yet we never truly forget them, and they are incredibly common. In fact, if you asked around you would be surprised how many people have some experience of magic. One of the most common examples is a premonition. When disasters strike it's often surprising how many people *didn't* go into work that day, or changed their schedule or route and thereby saved their lives. They may not be able to explain exactly why they did it – some may have had a clear premonition, while others made a split-second decision as though something was prompting them to avoid a tragedy.

Although Magic on the breath is a simple technique, like all things that are worth doing you have to work at it. Whatever sort of spell you do, whether it's for healing or protection, you're trying to influence events and/or people so you can obtain the results you want. You can read up all you like about such things, but there is a world of difference between wanting to learn about magic and actually casting a spell. In one of my magic workshops many years ago, someone once asked, 'Are there any spells I can do that don't require any work?' The simple answer of course, is no. To actually perform a spell involves a certain amount of effort and commitment.

Magic is often criticised because basically you are trying to get your own way with something. Even if you are performing a spell for someone else, it is still *your* intention as the spell-caster that goes into the spell. And this makes some people feel very uncomfortable with the whole idea of magic. They start accusing you of being selfish, but actually magic is no more selfish than so than many other things we do in the course of our lives. Most of the time – in the real world and the magical ones – we simply try to do the best we can for ourselves or for others. No more, and no less. That's not selfish. Remember that the opposite of selfish is not selfless but doormat. And in my experience doormats have a nasty habit of not only giving away their own rights but those of other people, too.

Magic is also sometimes accused of interfering with other people's free will. This is true up to a point, but plenty of other things in everyday life do the same thing. For example, if I drive on the left hand side of the road, anyone driving towards me is forced to drive on their left in order to avoid a head-on collision. Sometimes it's necessary to interfere with free will just to keep things moving!

Another accusation you will often hear is that magic is a form of cheating. Again, this is not true. If you want something badly it's natural to make an effort to give yourself the best chance. Revising for an exam will certainly give you an advantage, but it's not cheating unless you try and smuggle a text book into the exam room! Actually, I did once hear a student – who had failed his examination - claim that it was somehow more 'honourable' not to revise!

Taken to extremes, such ideas paralyse all attempts at magic. A good example of this is the claim that magic should only be used for the loftiest purposes. This attempt to claim the moral high ground can be very off-putting, making us feel that magic should be shut in a cupboard and only brought out - like the best china - for special occasions. That of course, is nonsense. Like anything else, magic requires training and practice in order to become competent and you can't do that if you won't even try! In fact, it's the ill thought-out, badly performed spells that cause most of the problems, not those that go strictly according to plan.

Getting to grips with magical ethics

How *do* we learn to distinguish between what's acceptable and what isn't? Who decides these things? Believe it or not, the answer is – us. And the more power we have, the more responsibility we have to use it well and not turn into a magical thug. Partly it's a question of attitude. There's a world of difference between wanting to pass your own exam and hoping everyone else will fail.

Most of us try to sensibly weigh up the pros and cons of casting a spell, and the old saying, 'Be careful what you pray for, you might get it,' holds particularly good for magic. For example, think about a toddler throwing a tantrum to get his own way in a supermarket. He wants sweets off the shelf, or a toy, and his parents say he can't have them. Perhaps they feel he has eaten enough sweets that day, or know he already has a box full of toys that he never plays with. If he has more sweets he will probably be sick. If he has yet another toy, it will probably not please him.

It's the same with magic. What you want isn't necessarily going to be good for you, and even if it's good for you it might not be good for those around you. What you need is some sort of code or rule to act as a guide and over the years people who perform magic have devised various mottoes, maxims and rules to try and ensure they (and others!) don't get carried away with *purely* selfish motives. Remember what you want for yourself is one thing. What you try and inflict on others is something else entirely.

One of the first rules you are likely to come across is a quotation from something called the Wiccan Rede, which is often quoted as, 'An it harm none, do what ye will.' It's often claimed to date back into antiquity, although it's probably no older than the late nineteenth century. Some people will try and insist that the Rede applies to *all* magic. It doesn't. It was only ever meant to apply to Wiccans, so if you're not Wiccan and don't intend becoming one, it doesn't have to apply to you. Of course the idea of 'harming none' is very appealing, although if you look at it a little more closely you'll realise it does have its problems.

'An it harm none, do what ye will.' What does it mean exactly? The usual interpretation is that provided you don't harm any-one you can cast whatever spells you like. Only of course, this has its drawbacks, because everything we do – even when it's with the best of intentions – has the potential to harm someone or something. Taken to extremes this can prevent you doing any magic whatsoever. So if, like me, you enjoy doing magic, you will probably need to find an ethical guideline that will not tie your hands so tightly. However, if you like the Rede then you can choose to be guided by it. It's up to you.

The next well-known saying you might come across is 'Do as thou wilt shall be the whole of the law.' Again this is a saying that has been plucked out of its full context, coming from the Book of the Law, by Aleister Crowley, a famous Thelemic magician. At first sight this maxim looks capable of justifying almost anything, and Crowley's critics have indeed accused him of teaching that we should all do exactly what we please without thought for the consequences.

However Crowley well understood that we do not live in a vacuum. Whatever we do is liable to have a knock-on effect with other people. Or as Crowley once expressed it in his book, *The Law is for All*, 'Unless one wants to wreck the neighbourhood, it is best to explode one's gunpowder in an unconfined space.' He also made a distinction between the 'true will' of a person and a mere whim, since absolute freedom brings with it absolute responsibility.

Another saying you will sometimes come across is 'What goes around comes around.' This can apply to many things, not just magic. And it's pretty sensible too, reminding us that there are all sorts of causes and effects that may eventually come back to haunt us.

The axiom I use – and which I strongly recommend for beginners - was handed down by witches in my family years ago. 'Wishes and curses are like old hens. They always come home to roost.' Chaucer uses a variant of it, back in the Middle Ages, and it has passed into the realm of proverbs as 'Curses are like hens, they come home to roost.' The version I learned however, has one important difference, 'Wishes and curses'. This emphasises that all magical practices – good or bad – have attendant risks. It's quite different from doing whatever you like and thinking it's enough to say 'sorry' afterwards.

Anyone who practices magic has to accept responsibility for their own actions. If you make a magical mess, even an unintentional one, it's your job to clean it up. And if you've ever tried clearing up magical fallout, you'll understand it's much simpler to take proper care before you cast a spell!

However, being prepared to take responsibility doesn't mean you should avoid all risks. Far from it. The choices we make in magic are much like those we face every day. For example, if you go out and get drunk on a Saturday night, you risk getting into a fight, being mugged, run down by a car or a host of other things. These aren't part of some mythical profit and loss account that's just waiting for you to do something wrong. These are sensible causes and effects. You can either (a) change your ways by going out but drinking moderately, (b) become a hermit and never go out at night again, or (c) continue unchecked and risk getting killed or seriously injured. The choice is yours. It's your life, your call. Just as it is when you cast a spell.

Asking permission before casting a spell
Another thing you'll often hear is that you should *always* ask the subject's permission before casting a spell and that it's quite unethical not to do so. This is simply not true, and is just yet another example of a very recent addition to magical practice claiming an authority it has never really deserved.

Ancient spells certainly never mention asking anyone's permission. People mostly just went ahead and cast their spells as they saw fit even though they sometimes trod a very fine line between what was legal and what was not. When it comes to asking permission all you need is a little common sense. For example, some people will claim that healing spells should never be carried out without first asking permission. Fair enough. But if you saw someone fall in the street, it would be natural to offer to help them up again. You wouldn't stand there saying, 'Excuse me, but do I have your permission to help you?' although you might say, 'Would you like some help?' But if you saw someone lying on the floor unconscious, would you really wait for their permission before calling an ambulance?

There's a time and place for everything, and usually in everyday life we can work this out as we muddle along. For example, you might well ask someone 'Would you like me to carry your shopping home for you?' because if you simply grabbed their bag they could think you were trying to rob them. It's the same with magic.

Often it's a good idea to bear in mind the old saying, 'As above, so below,' which comes from a famous alchemical work, the *Emerald Tablet of Hermes Trismegistus*. (The full quote is, 'As below, so above; and as above so below. With this knowledge alone you may work miracles.') If you apply the same principles to magic that you do to your everyday life, then you're unlikely to go very far wrong. There are times when it's sensible to ask permission, and times when it is merely polite. Only you can decide whether it's appropriate.

The Three Main Types of Spells
Although there are hundreds of different spells, there are three basic types:

1. Wishing spells
This is the largest group containing the most common type of spell, where you hope to achieve, deny or gain something either for yourself or for someone else. Almost all the most popular spells fall into this category, together with healings, wart charms, blessings and even hexes.

2. Entrusting spells
These are spells that entrust everything to whichever deities or powers you usually work with. They are useful when you really don't know what to do for the best but feel you should do *something*. If you find the

ethics of magic confusing or constraining, then entrusting spells may be your best option, at least in the early days.

3. Invocations/Evocations
Depending on your chosen spiritual path, you may find yourself using invocations and evocations to summon your chosen deity, spirit or entity. The two terms are often used interchangeably but have quite different meanings. When you invoke something, you are in effect inviting it within. This can be helpful if you want to get to know your chosen deity or entity. We can also invoke the spirits of certain festivals in order to help us understand their true meaning and enter into the spirit of them more fully.

When you evoke something, however, the divine being or spirit entity always remains apart and separate. Evocations are usually performed when the magician wishes to formally question the entity, perhaps in order to acquire new magical or spiritual knowledge (and sometimes to request the whereabouts of hidden treasure!). Evocations are usually associated with ceremonial magic, and are not really suitable for Magic on the Breath.

* * *

In my own experience I've found that the better I became at doing spells the less I needed them. Perhaps, in a perverse way, once we learn the mechanics of spell casting and can incorporate it into everyday life, the need for a special spell for a specific purpose disappears. In other words, magic no longer becomes unusual to us; it is there at our fingertips all the time. Instead of a spell, you have a magical mind-set. Doing magic is a bit like trying to tune into a radio station – sometimes you can't quite get a clear signal. And yet, because you know that the radio station is there, you keep trying. It's the same with magic. Keep practicing and it will eventually come through for you.

Chapter Two
First steps in breath control, grounding and visualisation

There are three basic magical techniques that we must master in order for our breath to support and send our magic out into the world: breathing, grounding and visualising. Normally we breathe without even thinking about it, but if we are going to use our breath for magical purposes, then we need to learn some specific techniques. These have other advantages too, since controlled breathing not only helps us ground and meditate, but also aids visualising. Without effective visualizing, magical work is little more than poetry or play acting.

Exercise 1 – Noticing your breath
This may sound obvious, but in fact it's very important to begin by making a few notes. These help chart your progress and highlight any areas that need extra work. Although it sounds ridiculously simple, I do urge you to give it a try. Begin by paying attention to what happens when you breathe. Notice how your chest rises and falls, perhaps even your shoulders or abdomen. Try and observe yourself breathing in a variety of different situations, not just walking, sitting, or lying down, but also when you're putting the laundry into the washing machine, driving, decorating, etc.

Next make a note of how emotions can affect your breathing too. In particular try and pay attention to how you are affected by stress, anger, sorrow and laughter. The more agitated we become, the quicker our breathing, and when people tell us to 'calm down' what they usually mean is that we should breathe more naturally. If we're very agitated we might even be told to breathe into a paper bag to prevent us from hyperventilating. But do *you* breathe more deeply or rapidly than usual? Remember there's no right or wrong answer to these questions, everyone is different. What matters is *your* response.

Next look at how the weather affects you. Do you breathe differently when it's cold and icy? I remember when I was a child playing at 'dragons' in winter, when I could see my breath streaming endlessly out in front of me. It was great fun and I was always amazed just how much 'breath' I could see. Yet on a hot summer's day I would feel my breathing had become shallow and rapid. In the same way animals pant to keep themselves cool in hot weather. Paying attention to such simple things is the key to understanding your breathing.

Now think about what it feels like when you breathe. How does breathing in feel different from breathing out? What happens when you try to take a really deep breath? What is the difference between taking a deep breath through the mouth and one through the nose? Which is easier? What does it feel like to be short of breath? Again, there are no right and wrong answers, just jot down your findings.

Exercise 2 - Getting your breathing under control

Now you have made notes about how you breathe in normal, everyday life you have a starting point. Next you need to learn how to control your breathing to make it do exactly what you want. To do this you have to experiment. For example, how long can you hold your breath? How quickly – and slowly – can you breathe in? How fast can you breathe out? All these things will affect your magic.

First of all, begin by standing in front of a mirror. Ideally you should position yourself to give a good view from the top of your head down to your waist. If this isn't possible you need to be able to at least see your head and shoulders. Now take a really deep breath and note whether your shoulders move (most people's do). However, for the purposes of magic you need to keep them absolutely still. This may take quite a bit of practice, but if you notice your shoulders moving when you breathe in then you aren't doing it properly - at least, not for the purposes of magic! But how do we stop our shoulders moving?

Begin by locating your diaphragm – that area above the navel and between the two racks of your ribs. Feel for it with the palm of your hands. When you breathe in you need to fill your lungs from the bottom upwards, rather like filling a bottle. The diaphragm should push *out* when we breathe *in*, and pull *in* as we breathe out – which is exactly the opposite of what most of us do if we're left to our own devices.

To help yourself breathe properly, try pressing the diaphragm *in* with your hands as you breathe *out*. Another method is to lie down on your back on a firm surface with a book placed on your abdomen. When you're breathing properly you'll see the book rise as you breathe in and fall as you breathe out. This way the body is squeezing out all the old stale air from the lungs. If you want to be sure that you completely empty your lungs when breathe out, just cough lightly.

Learning to breathe deeply using your abdomen and not your shoulders helps every part of you. It's like the difference between being out in the open air and shut up in a stuffy office all day long. It will also help you to ground yourself, mediate and visualise, all essential skills for magical work and spiritual growth.

Exercise 3 - Playing Games with your Breath

Once we've mastered the knack of breathing properly, the next thing is to start playing games with our breath. When we are young most of us have an innate gift for magic. Later, as we begin to try and analyze what we are doing, that instinctive talent is often smothered. Learning to play games with our breath is a way of reclaiming our magical talents by allowing our minds to relax as we explore the various breathing techniques.

For your first game, try breathing in through the nose to a count of four then out through the mouth to another count of four. For most of your work in Magic on the Breath, you'll need to breathe in through the nose and out through the mouth so this is good practice. You can even try it when you're out walking - your steps will help keep your counting steady and set up a rhythm. It also helps make journeys pass more quickly, especially if you breathe in and out for a count of seven!

When you've mastered this and are comfortable with it, try breathing in to a count of four and out to a count of eight. Then breathe in for four, hold for four, breathe out for four and hold for another four. Other things to try include breathing in for four counts, holding for four, and then breathing out to a count of eight and holding again for four. Once you've mastered this basic pattern, try and breathing in for four, holding for eight, breathing out for eight and then *holding again* for eight. Then try extending the count so you breathe in for five and out for ten or in for six and out for twelve etc. You should also experiment with shorter breaths such as counts of two in and four out, exhaling a little more forcefully to make sure you expel all the air. Don't be afraid to experiment, trying everything from gentle, barely there breathing to forceful gusts!

If you find some of these exercises a little difficult, practice building up the breath counts gradually. Just do what you feel comfortable with, and only increase the count very gradually. Remember to relax – being tense is not the same as having good self control and can actually interfere with our breathing.

Exercise 4 – Finding the Pulse in your Breath

Obviously there is more to breathing exercises than just standing there and solidly counting one…two…three… etc. Now you need to start looking for the inner rhythm. Think of it as a sort of pulse, a throbbing sensation within the breath that underlies your counting.

One of the easiest rhythms to feel is *one*-two–three; *one*-two–three with the stress on the first beat, rather like a waltz. Try a long, moderately forceful exhaled breath and see if you can make yourself feel this. You may need to 'push' slightly harder on the first beat as you breathe out, and less heavily on the second and third. (You can of course feel a pulse whether you inhale or exhale, but it's easier to feel on an exhaled breath.) Don't forget that the rhythm in our breath can also vary according to our mood. When we're agitated it speeds up, when we are calm it often slows right down. Practice feeling the pulse at different speeds, and take note of your mood whilst you do so.

If you still can't feel this pulse running through your breathing, try combining it with a simple two syllable word or phrase that you softly chant to yourself over and over again. Suitable words include things like 'Peaceful', or 'Be Still' for very relaxed breathing, and phrases like 'flow fast! ' or 'higher!' for when you want the rhythm to speed up. You don't need to feel the pulse on every single exhaled breath. Sometimes you'll need to take an extra breathe just to steady yourself before trying again, especially with quicker rhythms. Don't be afraid to experiment until you find what suits you best. Another method for feeling the various rhythms in your breath is to pay attention to your heartbeat at the end of each breath in and out. So you breathe in, feel the 'duh-duh' heart beat, then breathe out and feel the same 'duh-duh' rhythm just before you breathe in again. Once you've mastered this, try repeating the heartbeat rhythm for the entire length of the exhaled breath.

Exercise 5 – Breathing on the Vowels

Saying vowel sounds aloud is an ancient magical technique. It was particularly popular in ancient Greece and Egypt, and a magician who could perform the task properly was believed to be able to summon and control spirits by the tone of his voice alone. However, because such skills were passed down orally, the original technique has been lost. We cannot know exactly how it was done, and the sound of an English vowel may not be identical to what was said and sung in ancient Greece. However, vowels are the clearest sound in any language, so you can easily adapt the principle in your own magical work.

Basically all you do is take a deep breath using your diaphragm and without raising your shoulders. Then:

- On the out breath say softly 'Ah...'
- On the in breath say 'eh...' (like the 'e' in 'pet')
- On the following out breath say 'i ...'(as in 'ink')
- On the in breath say 'oh...' (as in 'hot')
- And finally breathe out for as long as you can, saying 'oo'.

Each breath should be roughly the same length and your voice needs to sound no louder than a whisper.

Then try swapping over the breaths, so that 'Ah' is said as you breathe in instead of out and so on. When you feel more confident try saying more than one vowel to each breath.

Exercise 6 – Candle Exercises

The basic principle of Magic on the Breath is that as we exhale, our breath will carry our magical intention out into the world. Therefore it stands to reason that the more control we have over our breathing the better. Candles are useful because their flames are sensitive to the slightest breeze, although obviously you need to observe sensible precautions and never leave them unattended.

For the first exercise, light a candle and set it in a holder on a on a solid surface (a table is ideal) so that the flame is about twelve to eighteen inches in front of your mouth. Then breathe out very gently aiming to empty your lungs *without blowing out the candle*. At first you may find you have to move the candle further away, but gradually you should be able to bring it closer (always being careful not to burn yourself.)

Next, practice breathing out on the word 'hah'. This should be little more than a whisper, and it helps you control your breath while speaking, which can be useful if you want to include spoken words in your magic (although actually it's not essential). Once you've mastered this, try breathing out on the five vowels (as you did in the previous exercise) without blowing out the candle flame. Experiment with the different distances, seeing how close you can bring the candle without extinguishing it.

Exercise 7 – Breathing on the Hand

Once you can control a gentle 'out' breath, you need to apply a little more force to it, breathing out through *slightly* pursed lips. Obviously a candle won't be suitable for this, so you need to wet a small area on the palm of your hand. Then hold your hand about six inches away from your mouth and breathe out. You will easily feel your breath because it will make the wet patch on your hand feel very cold.

Now move your hand a little further away and repeat the exercise. You should still be able to feel your breath, but perhaps not so strongly. The aim is not to 'huff, puff and blow the house down' but to produce a strong, constant stream of air on the exhaled breath.

Exercise 8 – First Steps in Grounding

Most of us value freedom of one sort or another, but we still need some point of reference as a means of keeping us safe. Without these we would be like clouds, forever wandering, unable to stop. We need stability, a fixed point, so that although we soar like eagles, we always have a means of getting back. This is particularly important in magical work, to avoid weakening the link between our psychic and physical self; you will often hear it referred to as 'grounding.'

Grounding can be as simple or complex as you choose, provided you observe some basic rules. Going back to the idea of 'As above, so below' in Chapter One, when you *physically* ground yourself, you're aware exactly how it feels to be connected to the earth. Once you can do this, you then remember and visualise that sensation whenever you need it.

But what *does* it feel like to be connected to the earth? Years ago, dedicated gardeners would drop their trousers and test whether the ground was warm enough to plant seeds by sitting on it with their bare bottoms! I'm not suggesting anything as extreme as this (besides, you could probably get yourself arrested) but at least kick your shoes off and go outside.

Since most of us live in towns and cities, the chances are that all your bare feet will have any contact with is concrete or paving slab, so you may need to find a small area of garden or parkland. Obviously you don't have to spend your life wandering round barefoot, but you should at least aim to experience the reality of standing on the earth before trying to visualize it. If you have chance to go to a beach, try going barefoot on the sand. And while you do these things keep asking yourself, 'What memories can I take away from this experience? What words and images will help me to remember?'

Once you've tried this a few times you should be able to close your eyes and remember what it feels like to be in contact with the earth. If you're still having difficulties, think of a few keys words to use as prompts while you are practicing out of doors. 'Sinking' could remind you of soft loam, 'dew' of wet grass in the morning and so on. And don't forget the *smell* of earth too. In summer it's baked hard by the sun, in autumn it's rich and sweet with the fallen leaves. The idea is to build a mental picture of what being in touch with the earth actually feels like so that later, when you're back indoors you can recreate -i.e. visualize – what it felt like. What did you smell, see, hear and touch? Practice regularly, writing down your observations in a notebook so that no matter where you are, you'll be able to ground yourself quickly and easily.

Exercise 9 – Grounding

So far you've been observing a real setting. But of course it's a big help if you can also imagine a setting too because you don't always have the luxury of being out of doors when you need to perform a spell. Some areas are easier to visualize than others. But even if you need to do magic on the top floor of a block of flats, the foundations of the building are deep in the earth, which means you're still connected to it, albeit indirectly. For this exercise you'll need find somewhere quiet where you will be undisturbed and can read the sections in italics in the following passage to yourself. Remember to pay attention to your breathing, keeping it gentle, relaxed and steady.

[Breathe out] *I am standing on the earth. It feels....* (Soft? Hard? Dew soaked? Dry crunchy leaves underfoot?) *I feel my hands reaching out deep into the earth, my fingers touch leaves, moss, blades of grass; my hands dig down deep into the earth.* (If possible, stretch out your hands, if not just imagine it. The most important thing is to create a sense of reaching out.) *It's surprising how soft it is, like a feather mattress. Deep, deep, deep into the earth.*

(The first few times you try this, you will probably run out of breath before you have finished. Don't worry, just take a quick breath and concentrate on breathing out again. With practice the whole thing can easily be accomplished on a single 'out' breath.)

[Breathe in]. *Now I draw up strength and power from the earth.* (As you breathe in either physically or mentally draw your arms back towards your body, so that your hands, palms facing your chest come to rest above your heart.) *Strength of the earth, be mine. Flood my body, heart and soul. Make me strong.*

Repeat this exercise a few times until you feel you can draw no more power into your body. Don't overdo it. Then breathe out softly a few times just to steady yourself before moving on to whatever magical work you intend doing.

This exercise can also be useful for steadying yourself before any stressful event, such as an interview or examination. For magical work, I prefer to ground first, although I know some people prefer to ground themselves afterwards and a few stalwarts like to do it before *and* after.

Try the exercise a few times as it is before adapting it to suit your own personal needs. For example, if the idea of reaching into the earth doesn't work for you, then look for something that does. I once had a friend who couldn't bear the idea of putting her hands into the earth because she was terrified of creepy crawlies. Eventually we hit on the idea of using the imagery of the sea instead, because she was particularly attuned to the element of water. So as the waves rolled in she would imagine herself drawing up strength and power, and as they drew back again she would feel herself reaching out deep into the wet sand. Don't be afraid to experiment!

Grounding stones

Whilst on the subject of grounding, this is a good place to mention grounding stones which can be a useful tool if you find grounding difficult. Any smooth pebble that's small enough to hold in the palm of your hand while performing your grounding exercise will do. Some people like to mark their grounding stones with signs from the zodiac, runes or a pentagram. Personally I prefer to leave mine blank; stones are beautiful enough without my scribbling all over them, but that's just my personal preference.

Before using a grounding stone you'll need to cleanse it. Some people like to leave it out under a full moon, or outside in the sunshine, while those who are in more of a hurry will simply ring a bell over it. You can also breathe out over it several times, mentally willing it to be clean. Once cleansed, it can be held whenever you ground yourself as a physical token and reminder of the earth.

You can also use grounding stones to soothe you at times of stress. The more you do this, the more the stone itself will become charged with negativity; you'll notice that it becomes dull and unpleasant to touch. When this happens all you have to do is cleanse it again. It's often a good idea to keep a couple of stones so you can use one while the others are being recharged. They always seem to feel better when they have been left out in the sun or moonlight for a day or two!

Visualisation

Many people worry unnecessarily about visualisation. In fact we visualise things every day without even realising it. For example, we sometimes imagine how our lives would be if we won the lottery, became a film star or lived in a big house. Years ago people called it day dreaming, and it was very much discouraged since it tended to make people impractical and unrealistic.

However, the odd day dream can be a useful escape valve for dealing with the drudgery of everyday life. Many a downtrodden clerk or shop assistant copes with their lot in life by imagining exotic and exciting lifestyles in their daydreams. There are worse things they could be doing.

We are all born with vivid imaginations. Small children create imaginary friends for themselves without any help from the adults around them. It's only as we grow up that our imaginations become stifled, usually by other people. So it's little wonder that when we attempt visualisation for magical purposes, we often panic and give up altogether.

Part of the problem is that we try too hard. Shutting our eyes, tensing up, trying to focus on things we don't quite understand...it's no wonder so many of us fail. But it doesn't have to be like that. In fact, the more laid-back you are, the better. The next few exercises use simple visualization techniques to help spring clean and revitalize our minds.

Exercise 10 – Getting Rid of Mental Clutter - Shame

Most of us have a load of mental clutter in our heads somewhere: old emotional baggage, hang-ups, all the detritus of life that has probably been hanging around for years. It may be tucked away in dark corners, or spilling out over the floor. We may even have become so used to the mess that we no longer really notice it's there. Unfortunately, unless we do something about it, it will interfere not only with our efforts to cast spells and do magic but with the very essence of our lives.

So, what sort of clutter can we expect to find and how can we deal with it? All mental clutter is riddled with negativity of one sort or another, and one of the most powerful forms of negativity is shame. It's a curious emotion. It may sound rather passive but in fact it can be hugely destructive. Shame paralyses us, often through no fault of our own, and worse, others will sometimes use it as a way of manipulating us. When that happens people are made to feel so ashamed of themselves – even if what happened wasn't their fault - that they can never let it go so they can get on with a normal life.

Firstly you need to find a quiet spot where you will be undisturbed for about ten minutes. Establish a comfortable relaxed pattern of breathing, in through the nose and out through the mouth. Now think of all the past occasions when people have tried (and succeeded!) in making you feel ashamed. You'll feel uncomfortable here, but please persevere, using your breathing to steady yourself. As you examine every instance of shame, acknowledge how it made you feel, and then imagine you have a large rubber stamp marked 'Paid.' Use this stamp mentally to mark the end of your debt to shame.

If you find visualising too hard or too painful, write down very briefly what happened. It could be a single word 'Clothes' 'Family' or 'Love' for example. Just enough so that you know what you mean. Then write 'Paid' across the words in capital letters. Finally rip the sheet into shreds or burn it. Place the pieces or ashes into a bag with some salt before placing it with the rubbish or casting it into running water.

I do understand that this exercise is very painful because shame reduces our self confidence until we feel insignificant and worthless.

For our spirit's own well being however, we have to try and break free. Nobody can hope to perform magic successfully with the dark shadow of shame hanging over them constantly. It has to be banished once and for all, and you'll be surprised how much better you'll feel afterwards.

Exercise 11 – Getting Rid of Mental Clutter – Learn to Stop Needing Approval

Mental clutter isn't always caused by things that have happened in the past. Sometimes it's just a bad habit we seem unable to break, such as continually looking to other people for their approval. Like many things, this has its roots in our childhood. Our first steps, our first words, the early pictures we paint in school and our end of term reports - we always hope our parents will praise us for our efforts. And when they do it makes us feel warm and glowing inside.

Unfortunately, looking for praise from others becomes a habit for some people. When their parents have deliberately withheld praise or are no longer there to praise us, we seek it from others. If we find it perhaps in a partner or friend, all well and good. If we don't, it's easy to reach the stage where we're seeking praise from anyone. Anyone at all. This attitude not only makes us vulnerable but is the kiss of death to magical work, which requires a level of quiet confidence in our own abilities.

So, for this exercise practise praising yourself. Banish phrases like 'Just my luck,' or 'This always happens to me,' from your vocabulary. There is no reason you should have worse luck than anyone else. But if you act as though that's what you deserve then that is almost certainly what you will get.

Try looking in the mirror and instead of looking for blemishes, weight gain and wrinkles, pick out your good points. Believe me, you'll have plenty. Now say them over to yourself, nodding as you do so. Smile at yourself in the mirror. Tell yourself that you're doing well. Mirrors are complex entities that can reflect back our inner feelings in ways we would never expect. Start telling your mirror how much you like yourself and suddenly you'll notice that the mirror likes you, too. Give it a try – you'll be pleasantly surprised.

Exercise 12 – Getting Rid of Mental Clutter – Learning not to Fear Criticism

That great writer of ancient fables, Aesop, told a story of a man and his son who tried to please everyone and ended up pleasing nobody, least of all themselves. That should be a lesson to all of us. There is nothing wrong in pleasing ourselves. It's not an *inherently* bad thing to do. Obviously, it can be taken to extremes and abused, but so can many other things. Giving someone a piece of cake can be a gesture of hospitality; force feeding them nothing but cake for three months could be considered cruel.

Along with not looking for approval we need to stop looking over our shoulder wondering whether people are criticising us. Like shame, criticism can be a powerful weapon. If you someone you care about makes you feel guilty enough, they will soon control your every move. For example, often we're told that if we follow a certain course of action people 'won't like you,' or will 'talk about you.' What this means in effect is that a group of faceless, unknown people have somehow been allowed to take charge of our lives, and dictate our actions. But who are these people? Who gave them this awe-inspiring authority? Why should we accept it anyway?

It's important to understand that none of us can expect to be liked by everyone all the time. And not all approval is equally desirable. Frankly there are some people I would rather *didn't* like me. Would you want someone like Hitler to think you were an all round great person? Of course not. So if you don't want the friendship or approval of someone you dislike, then why should you crave it from the faceless 'they'? After all, you don't even know whether their approval is worth having!

Remember too that the opposite of selfish is not selfless, kind or even generous. The opposite of selfish is *doormat* because both are extremes. I am not suggesting for one minute that our lives should be one long hedonistic spree of self indulgence; but neither do I think long suffering martyrdom necessarily makes us better people. Most of the 'martyrs' I've ever met will give you the shirt off their back – but will make you pay for it for the rest of your life.

For this exercise you need to examine the things you do in your daily life that are done solely in order to conform. This may be the way you dress, the things you eat, say or think. Allow yourself a few days to make a list, and then decide which ones you could change. It's unlikely you'll ever change them all – sometimes they are necessary in order to keep down a job or stay on speaking terms with the family. But there will be some where you can make a stand, however small it happens to be. You're not trying to antagonise others, just trying to make a statement about your own identity.

Make the changes gradual. If you suddenly want to dress all in black, try adding one black item at a time to your wardrobe. That way it is easier and you can just ease yourself into it gradually. Instead of doing things in the hope that others will somehow be pleased, you will quite literally, please yourself. And people who are at ease with themselves cast better, stronger spells.

Exercise 13 – Spring-cleaning the mind

Now that you've pinpointed some of the likely obstacles to your emotional well being, you can get on with the mental Spring cleaning. You'll be pleasantly surprised how much easier magic will be once you get rid of the clutter.

Begin by finding somewhere quiet to sit where you will not be disturbed for at least five minutes. Ground yourself and then establish an easy, relaxed breathing pattern - in through the nose and out through the mouth. Now mentally envisage yourself getting rid of old grudges, old hurts, all the barriers that are preventing you from moving on with your life. These have taken a lifetime to accumulate so don't expect to get rid of them all at a stroke. Some will require a great deal of effort and determination; others will go quietly once you show them the door. You will probably have to be quite ruthless.

For example, yes, it was painful that your boyfriend dumped you five years ago, but surely you need to move on now? And that job that didn't work out the way you'd hoped, it didn't really blight your life forever, did it? Just acknowledge that these things hurt at the time, but now let them go. Mentally imagine opening windows and allowing dark thoughts and memories fly away forever.

You will probably find this exercise quite exhausting both mentally and emotionally, so don't spend too long it. Instead, aim for little and often. It's better to do just five minutes once a day than spend an hour once a week only to end up feeling completely frazzled.

Exercise 14 – Beginning Visualization

Once your mind is clear, you'll find visualisation much easier. Even so, you should come to it without any expectations. Relax and enjoy the process of seeing and yet not seeing which is really what visualising in all about. Use your imagination and create whole worlds for yourself, remembering to treat it as play, not work. You should aim to use all your five senses in visualising – it's not just about seeing, it's also about 'recreating' old experiences using every available means at your disposal.

Let's suppose we're going to visualize a cat. If you want to you can use a cat you've known as a template for your visualized cat. First you must decide what sort of cat it will be, the breed, gender, temperament, approximate age and appearance.   Then consider how your other senses will react to this creature. What will it sound like? Some cats are more vocal than others and make all sorts of strange noises. Does it purr at your touch?   What does its coat feel like when you stroke it? What does it smell like? (Of course it doesn't have to be a cat. If you prefer you can choose an animal you *have* had some experience of.)

Remember that you are aiming to recreate a 'virtual' creature, in three dimensions. Imagine seeing it from different angles, mentally walking round it or watching it walk around you. Most beginners make the mistake of trying too hard and too long when they begin to visualise something. Most spells can be done quite quickly so you don't need to spend an entire morning visualizing, and you'd probably go mad if you tried. Just begin with a few minutes and try to gradually increase it to five or ten.   If you begin to feel light-headed then stop, do your grounding exercise and take a few days' break from visualisation work before trying again.

If you do have to take a break, remember that you can always pick up again where you left off. You don't have to return to the beginning every time you visualise something. With practice you can even use visualisation to create thought forms, a type of magic that is dealt with more fully in Chapter Five.

Exercise 15 – Improving self confidence

The level of success we can achieve in magic depends largely on our ability to 'bend' the will of the cosmos, or at least give it a shove in a favourable direction. At the very least therefore, when you begin a spell, you must have a reasonable expectation of its success. Look at football managers, they never tell the press that their team doesn't have a snowball's chance in hell of winning the FA Cup, instead they go out there and say that the players are 'in with a good chance'.

It must be the same when you do a spell, otherwise your own self doubt will work against you. Unfortunately, this also means that people who are brimming with self confidence to the point of are likely to have more initial success in their magic, even though their intentions may be more selfish. So if you feel that you are lacking in self esteem, or naturally shy, you should add the following exercise to your regular daily rituals.

For your magic to work well – not matter what method you use - you have to believe in it and in yourself. This is no time for false modesty. If you start off with a negative view of yourself, a lot of that negativity will pass into your magic where, if it doesn't disable it completely it will certainly weaken it. I've met people whose self image was so low they had all but made themselves invisible. It's no good trying to do magic if you honestly believe you have no right to tell anyone to do anything. In magic you are attempting to influence chance, by bending the laws of nature and probability. If you view yourself as a shrinking violet or eternal wallflower, now is the time to do something about it.

So first of all, go out of doors to a place where you have a fairly good view all around you. Open countryside is ideal, but so is a local park, a beach, even a quiet car park. The first time you do this exercise you will probably find it easier if there is quite a bit of space around you, but later on it can be practiced anywhere.

Imagine yourself as the central point of a circle, and then imagine the line of its circumference. It can be as large as you like, the only proviso is that you must be the only person in your circle, and you must be at its centre. This can mean mentally juggling the size of your circle until you get it right. Then, turn clockwise, very slowly, until eventually you are back facing where you began, all the time observing what is around you and within your circle. It doesn't have to be a beautiful view, the important thing is to impress upon yourself that you are the centre of this world.

When you breathe for this exercise, keep your lips pursed as though you are about to whistle, but don't make any sound, just concentrate on breathing out in a long, narrow stream. Imagine that this breath can only travel to the edges of your circle, and that when it reaches the edge it turns around in a clockwise direction, cleansing as it goes. Sometimes in the beginning it helps to think of it as coloured smoke!

Before the first breath mentally say something like, 'With my breath I am going to clear away negativity and anxiety' or whatever is on your mind at the time. This is a very old magical technique known as a performative intention. You find something similar in the old wedding service 'With this ring, I thee wed.' You don't have to say it aloud, but you do at least have to think it clearly.

You will probably have to repeat this several times – about five - in fairly quick succession. The idea is that your breath cleanses the area around you, and thereby heals your lack of confidence. You can repeat this exercise as often as you want throughout the day, but as your self confidence increases you will find you need it less and less. It's the magical equivalent of spring cleaning your immediate environment.

Another thing that the exercise does is to remind us is that no matter where you are or what you're doing, you can be the centre of your own world. It can be a vast area if you stand on top of a mountain peak or a mere few feet if you happen to be sitting at your desk, but it is your world, and you are its centre. In this world of your personal space there is no room for the faceless 'they' to dominate your behaviour or thinking – this is your world, not theirs.

Some people also find it helpful to draw a visual reminder of this exercise in their magical notebook. A stick figure at the centre of a circle will do perfectly well, although you could pin a small photograph of yourself in the centre of a piece of paper and then draw a circle around that.

You can adapt this exercise further if you wish. For example, if you are feeling particularly fragile try visualising the circle becoming a bubble that extends around, above and below you. Think of it as your own, personal hamster ball. You can go where you like and the bubble goes with you. This bubble should be no more than a yard or so in every direction with you at the centre. It is totally clear, so you can see, smell and hear perfectly.

Unlike the circle which simply acts as a boundary marker, this bubble is completely sealed and sacrosanct – a magical HazMat suit. Nobody and nothing can touch you here. It doesn't impede your activities in any way, it doesn't damage or flatten anything. Its sole purpose is to protect. It's often a good way of coping in places where there is a great deal of negativity that you cannot clear by yourself.

Once you have worked your way through the exercises in this chapter and feel confident with them, you're ready to move on to exercises designed to develop your magical mind. Remember that success in magic depends upon focus. Never allow yourself to be distracted by hopes of praise or fear of censure.

Magic is your business, nobody else's.

Chapter Three
Working with the mind

It's perfectly possible to do magic long before you understand how it works. In fact some people have been excellent spell-casters all their lives without ever really getting to grips with the actual mechanics of magic. This shouldn't surprise us; after all, I switch on lights in my house everyday without properly understanding how electricity works. Likewise although I can use the telephone I can't tell you how it enables me to talk to people in another country or continent.

For some people however, magic is all about ritual and magical tools. They feel that as long as they have the 'right' crystal, or the 'right' incense, their spells are assured of success. In fact, what magic requires most of all is the power inherent in our minds, the intention or will. If you can control that, then you can do magic without any tools at all. If you cannot control it, your magic will be at best a pale shadow of what it could have been.

Unfortunately, we only use a small fraction of our brain power in everyday life. It's like having a powerful computer and only ever typing shopping lists on it. But most people don't even suspect their own potential, apart from odd occasions when they receive a very strong premonition or dream. All that power just shut away doing nothing. Don't you ever wonder what would happen if we could not only find it, but learn to control it?

Well, first we have to find a way to access all this power that seems to be hiding out in each of us. Some call it the subconscious, inner or unconscious mind; others describe it as the higher or inner self. The important thing is not what we call it, but that we know it exists within us. With most of us, our inner mind is probably bored rigid for 98% of the time, and this is our own fault because we've been ignoring it for years. Instead of trusting our instincts, or better still, trying to develop them, we fall back on gadgets and technology. Of course, from time to time it wakes up and sends a prophetic dream or premonition, but little else. Yet if you gave it half a chance you would be amazed what it could do. The trouble is, we have neglected it for so long we're not sure how to communicate with it anymore and it's become so accustomed to being ignored that it won't do anything unless it's a little out of the ordinary. Something our 'everyday' mind would never dream of doing. We have to wake it up.

Exercise 1 – Giving our Inner Mind something to do

For our first exercise, try guessing the total bill whenever you go shopping. It sounds simple and it is. But it is also very effective, because most of us don't use numbers in this way. Remember you're not trying to 'guesstimate' the bill, just taking the first number that pops into your head.

Next, try guessing the number of hits you will get on an internet search engine. Use really weird combinations in your search, for example, 'patience' with 'kippers' or 'horseshoe' with 'ambiguous'. The two exercises complement each other because they deal with such widely differing numbers. With shopping your guesses are likely to be less than fifty pounds, whereas with the internet exercise you could be dealing with hundreds or tens of thousands of hits.

Aim to do these exercises several times each day. After a while you'll notice that your guesses start becoming more accurate. This is a good sign because it means that your inner mind is beginning to wake up and show some interest. And that's a start.

Exercise 2 – Working with Time

Although it can be measured precisely, time is a very abstract concept for most of us. We talk about having a 'long day' or say that 'time flies when you're enjoying yourself' even when it's obvious that a day is always the same length and that a clock does not speed up the moment it hears you laugh.

So for this exercise you need to try and guess the time throughout the day. Go without a watch for a day or two, and resist the temptation to keep checking any clocks. This exercise works particularly well when you're out of doors – go back inside afterwards to check how close your guess was. After a while you begin to find you get a surprisingly accurate 'feel' for time. This is because your inner self *always* knows the time – we just never ask it!

Don't be put off by the apparently simplicity of these exercises. They are important because they use everyday things to help us access a deeply hidden aspect of our own nature. And they work.

Exercise 3 – Guessing with People

This is another exercise you can try without anyone having the slightest idea what you're doing. Simple try and guess the first word someone will say at any given moment. It doesn't even have to be anyone you know, the choice is yours. In fact often strangers are easier to work with because you are relying solely on your inner mind and not relying on what you *think* they might say at any given time.

At first you'll find that some people are easier to predict than others. Some will be virtually impossible. Please don't let this put you off. Persevere and you'll be surprised how much more accurate you'll become. This is because the more you trust and get to know your inner mind, the more it will work for you. I'm well aware that these three exercises may seem little more than children's games, but they are an excellent way of accessing this inner psychic space where true magic can begin. And once you become good at them, you can begin to make subtle adjustments. There's a very fine line between predicting what someone will say and actually influencing them to say what you want.

And this brings us to the ethics of magic. Obviously, although it's fun to bend others to your will, it does have its dark side. People will tell you that you should never rush into magic without first considering other options and ideas. This is good, practical advice. If there's an easier way of doing something, then you should certainly consider it.

Many beginners reach for a spell no matter what the problem, and so alas, do some people who have been practising magic for several years. Sometimes magic *is* the only way to deal with a situation but not always. It's important to look at all practical solutions first. Often these will do the trick, although sometimes you might need to give them a little magical boost to help them along.

In Chapter 1 we looked at the main types of spell, now it's time to look at some of them more closely and see how they can be used.

Wishing spells

These are probably the most common type of spell and basically fall into two main groups: spells to obtain or achieve something and spells to deny. This might seem to be stating the blatantly obvious but sometimes there's a very thin line between the two. For example, a protective spell would obviously fall into the first group because it keeps the subject of the spell safe. In other words, it achieves safety.

However, a spell to banish something, such as an entity, could belong to either group. It could belong in the first group, because it achieves spell caster's intention which is to banish the entity, or it could belong in the second group because it denies the entity what it wants (which is presumably to not be banished.)

If you have a situation where you want to achieve or deny something, then basically you use a wishing spell.

Entrusting spells

The main focus of this type of spell is to entrust everything to your deities or the power you work with. Some people like to state the desired outcome but not the method while others feel happier leaving all the decisions to the gods. They are particularly popular with people who want justice but draw the line at curses and hexing. Sometimes they all overlap; for example many of the old lead curse tablets used throughout the Roman Empire were a form of entrusting spell.

Invocations

Like entrusting spells, invocations call upon a deity or higher power. Sometimes the request is for protection, blessings or healings, rather like wishing spells. However invocations can also be performed to invite or even force a deity or power to enter into the magician. People are often surprised to find that traditionally magicians used a certain amount of coercion when dealing with entities, whether demonic or angelic, and even with deities. Personally I wouldn't recommend coercive invocations unless you are both experienced and confident. This is not the type of magic that is kind to ditherers.

What type of spell do you want to do?

Virtually all spells rely on one of two very basic techniques: they either draw something towards you or drive it away. So if you want to bring something into your life, you do a spell that draws the desired result to you. This includes invoking entities, since you are trying to make them approach. If you want to deny or get rid of something, you send it away. This also includes entrusting spells, where you are sending the entire problem to your deities or higher power. Once we know the intended direction of the spell it's fairly easy to use the appropriate breathing techniques to support our magic.

Of course in everyday life, your options do not always fall neatly into these clear cut categories. For example, your son is being bullied at school. Perhaps your first instinct would be to do a spell to curb the bullying. That would be a wishing spell intended to deny something by sending the bully's activities away. Or it could be intended to bring safety to your child.

Another alternative is a spell to ensure that some other person, perhaps a teacher, witnessed the bullying and intervened to stop it. In this instance you would be sending the teacher to the right place at the right time. Or you could to a spell to attract justice towards your child. If you did a spell to strengthen your child so it was easier for him to stand up for himself and give as good as he got you would need a spell to draw strength *towards* him. Alternatively you could do a spell to move the bully to another school.

As you can see, an apparently simple problem doesn't always have a simple remedy. The easiest way to begin is to work out exactly what you want from your magic. At its most basic level you want to protect your child. You then work backwards from this goal to find the best method to use.

Other situations might be more complicated. For example, suppose my neighbours are rather noisy, allowing their young child to have the television on full blast late into the night. Firstly I have to decide whether this is deliberate and whether it is aimed at me personally or someone else - it's quite possible the neighbours are actually trying to annoy each other. Also, we need to ask does it happen every night, or only sometimes? A problem caused by thoughtlessness is not going to require the same solution as one caused by malice. And an occasional problem is going to need a different approach from a near constant one.

In a situation like this, we also need to consider how the problem came about and who else is likely to be affected by it. Presumably the noise is disturbing the parents just as much as it affects me so why are they allowing it to happen? Do they have to get up for work the following day? If not, they may not mind so much. Or it may be that the child is a poor sleeper. Desperate parents may resort to anything to keep a wakeful infant occupied. Stupid parents may not care what the child is doing. And drunken parents may not even notice.

The reason I lay so much stress on the root causes and intent is because they affect how we approach the problem. Sometimes you try and improve situations by casting a spell on someone else. At other times you try and change your own consciousness, so that you can, in effect, sleep through all the noise. In this situation, there are several options if you decide to cast a spell:

1. You cast a spell to give the child a good night's sleep.
2. You cast a spell to make the parents (and child) more considerate, so that whatever their problems, they find a quieter solution to them.
3. You cast a spell to make you less aware of what they are doing; to give *yourself* a better night's sleep.

The first two spells are wishing spells to achieve something, the final spell works by denying yourself awareness of what is happening.

It may also be worthwhile to tackle any negativity that may be present. Often this can be what is really keeping the child awake into the early hours of the morning. Negativity can be present in both places and people, and small pockets of it are virtually everywhere. Most are too small to do much harm, but when these pockets cluster together into a great block they can and do cause a range of problems. These include persistent vague illnesses, headaches and sudden outbursts of weeping or anger. Once you know what to look for, you will start noticing strong areas of negativity, which often appear as a slight shadowing of the light. Even if you can't see it, you can certainly feel it as a heaviness in the atmosphere, and in extreme cases it feels like a lead weight on your head, chest and shoulders.

While I'm not convinced that negativity can ever be completely destroyed, I have found the following method useful for breaking it down into manageable chunks which will then disperse by themselves. Obviously you can't go into your neighbour's home to banish their negativity, but you can certainly go there mentally while remaining physically grounded on your own side of the fence!

This basic spell uses no words and is done through a combination of breathing and will; its strength comes entirely from you, and your intention. The more you practice, the more effective you will be. It's a very useful exercise for diffusing a wide variety of tense situations.

Exercise 4 – Dealing with Negativity

To deal with strong negativity you need to make a mental sweeping action in the shape of a figure-of-eight lying on its back or its side. Think of a large number eight chalked on the floor or sideways on a wall. Interestingly, in some traditions the figure eight shape laid on its side is an ancient symbol for dispersing negative energies. If the negativity is really heavy and dense you could even envisage it alternating between the two positions. Negativity is usually stagnant rather than mobile, so making it move helps break it up and weaken it.

Start off by imagining you're holding an old-fashioned besom brush (the traditional witches' broom!) To use it effectively you have to make a slightly curved movement whereas with an ordinary sweeping brush you use a straight back and forth motion. Now imagine yourself sweeping in this figure of eight pattern, through the air, anywhere you sense the negativity, and vigorously brushing the atmosphere until it is clean. If you find this difficult to visualise, simply get a sweeping brush or even a stick, find a quiet corner and try to physically make the appropriate sweeping motions. Observe your movements carefully so that you can recreate them in your visualisation. Ask yourself: *How does it make me feel? How does it sound?*

Now put the brush down and re-create this sweeping process mentally. It may require several attempts before you can do it at will, so persevere. Sometimes it can help to shut your eyes while visualising because this blots out the physical world and helps us concentrate on the magical one.

Once you can visualise the action, complete the ritual by paying attention to your breathing. All the power will be carried on the exhaled breath because *that comes from you.* It will take your intention out into the world, breaking up the negativity. As you work, you need to keep your head very straight and your mind focused; visualise your lower jaw parallel to the ground and tuck the tip of your tongue just behind your bottom front teeth. This will help keep your mouth and airway open and relaxed.

As your mind envisages the sweeping movement breaking up the negativity, start breathing out taking breaths whenever you need them. You need a firm but gentle force behind the outward breath, as if you're blowing on a candle from about eighteen inches away to make the flame flicker. If you're not sure what this is like, go and get a candle and practice the sort of breath you will need before continuing with breaking up the negativity.

This spell is not only useful for dispersing negativity in places but also for dealing with people who seem to carry their own personal black cloud around with them. Simply visualise sweeping clean the area all around them, paying particular attention to a direct line between you and them. It's also worth dispersing negativity in any physical space associated with them, such as a favourite chair or room.

You may have to repeat this exercise several times until things calm down, especially if a lot of anger has been generated. Remember that anger feeds off itself. The more anger is around the more powerful it grows, gathering momentum very quickly indeed.

Exercise 5 – Psychic Cleansing using a bell
Psychic cleansing is a very important skill. It's particularly important to psychically cleanse any area where you've dispersed negativity to ensure you get rid of any psychic debris left hanging around. It can also be used just before someone comes home from hospital or after a heated argument.

There are several ways to perform psychic cleansing. One of the easiest is to ring a bell. Pure sound is extremely effective because it literally makes the air (and nearby objects) vibrate for a long time afterwards. Work methodically over the area you wish to cleanse, remembering that the smaller the bell, the smaller the area it cleanses, so you will need to ring it more often than a larger one. After each ringing, if you stretch out your hand you should feel your fingertips tingling. If you live with people unaware of or unsympathetic to your magical practices try tapping a spoon against a glass instead. This produces a nice, clear bell-like sound.

As you ring the bell, breathe in to a count of three, hold for three, breathe out to six and hold for another three. As you exhale, visualise yourself literally blowing away any psychic debris from the original negativity. You will need quite a forceful breath for this, and should also ring the bell three times whilst holding your breath.

Exercise 6 – Psychic Cleansing using Incense
Incense can also be used for psychic cleansing. Although joss sticks are very popular and easy to use, in my experience you get better results (but a lot more smoke!) with incense burned on a solid charcoal block in a heatproof container. You can buy ready-made incense mixtures that include resins, herbs, leaves, wood shavings and flowers chosen for their magical properties. However, there is no reason why you can't make your own if you prefer, and you can use dried kitchen herbs such as sage and rosemary in the mixture. Rosemary makes a strong, clean smelling smoke and was traditionally burned as incense, hence its popular name of *Encensier* in France. It is ideal for psychic cleansing.

The same breathing pattern can be used while burning incense as you did while ringing a bell. If you use a joss stick you can focus on gently breathing out over the small glowing tip to encourage more smoke. However, with incense the exhaled breath should be fairly gentle, and you may need to refer back to the earlier exercises with the candle flame in order to obtain the correct strength. If you are using sold block incense, breathe on the charcoal block instead.

Charcoal blocks are a little fiddlier to use than joss sticks but once you get the hang of them they're quite simple. They are particularly good for areas that need thorough cleansing, but not so suitable if you want to walk around a room or through the home. Remember to place the heatproof container on a solid surface as close to the area to be cleansed as possible. Hold the solid charcoal disc so that its edge burns in a candle flame. In my experience it's safest to use kitchen tongs for this.

The charcoal will crackle and eventually start to glow red at one edge. Hold it in the flame a few more minutes before placing it carefully in its fireproof container. Then gradually add *small* amounts of herbs, woodchips and resin etc. Do not leave the incense unattended and remember that solid charcoal can take some time before it burns to ash so allow plenty of time for this ritual.

As you are about to add the herbs, resins, etc., to the block, you should exhale through slightly pursed lips in a long steady stream, being careful not to blow so hard that you risk scattering all the dried flower heads and woodchips! As the smoke begins to rise, concentrate on visualising it cleansing the space around you. Think of it as magical spring cleaning. You don't physically have to clean anything (although negativity does have an unpleasant habit of clinging to dust and grease). What you *must* do however, it so visualise everything as becoming spotless as you work.

If you find this type of visualisation difficult, it can help to have a mental library of strong 'clean' images that you can easily remember. I find it useful to think of clean, sparkling windows, polished metal, gleaming wood, anything dust free and essentially clean. Others might think of polishing brass or silver, or even spotlessly clean laundry! So you breathe out, and visualise all the negativity being blown, polished or washed away.

If the area to be cleansed is out of doors, try burning the herbs on a small, controlled bonfire, using the same breathing technique, and visualising the area being physically cleaned until it sparkles. One image you might find helpful is sweeping the path until there isn't a speck of dust left. Burning herbs on bonfires was traditional in northern Europe on St Thomas' Eve (the night before the Winter Solstice); Christmas Eve; New Years Day; Epiphany (6th January); Beltane and the Midsummer Solstice. When I was young people would also cast salt on the kitchen fire when they wanted to drive evil away.

Exercise 7 – Psychic cleansing using blessed water
If burning any sort of incense or lighting a bonfire is out of the question, don't despair. Just sprinkle the area to be cleansed with a sprig of rosemary (or some other plant with cleansing properties) dipped in blessed water.

Blessing something is itself a magical act and blessed water is simply ordinary tap water over which you perform a very simple blessing ceremony. You might prefer to collect fresh rainwater, or bring home water from a mountain stream, but for magical purposes it's still just water. Whatever you choose, don't be tempted to pay for ready-made 'blessed water'; it contains nothing you cannot do for yourself.

Simply collect your water in a clean glass container such as a well-washed jam jar. Begin – as always – by grounding yourself, then breathe in and hold your breath while reciting something like, 'I bless this water and everything it touches' or 'Blessed be this water and all it touches.' Then breathe out onto the surface of the water so that you send your intention and your words into the water. Try to use a 'warm breath' the sort you use when you want to make a mirror mist up.

If you have no privacy to speak aloud then simply say the words mentally to yourself. These can be as fancy or plain as you choose, although in my experience the simpler and more direct the better. You certainly shouldn't worry about making things rhyme. This is magic, not poetry! Some people like to invoke the deities they work with and ask them to help with the blessing, although strictly speaking this isn't essential. You can also add a pinch of salt as part of the ritual, although if you decide to use sea water you can omit that.

If you need to bless water for a specific person or magical intention then the wording should be along the lines of, 'I empower you to bless *[name or magical intention]*.' Remember though that water blessed in this way can *only* be used for or by the person named, or for the magical intention you have stated. If you need blessed water for anything else you will require a fresh batch. Water which has been generally blessed can be used for a variety of purposes.

Next dip a sprig of rosemary, box, oak, pine, juniper, sage or any other protective herb of your choosing into the water and sprinkle the area you wish to cleanse. Remember to breathe in as you dip the spring into the water and out as you flick the water away from you. You can use quite a firm out-breath for this, especially when working out of doors.

Now that you have learned some of the basic skills for practising Magic on the Breath, it's time to go looking for the magic that surrounds us...

Chapter Four

The Magic that Surrounds Us...

Magic can be a lonely business. For centuries it was persecuted almost into the ground. Folk or 'low' magic in particular was forced to be very careful because its practitioners were mostly ordinary people without powerful patrons to protect them. Since few people could read or write before the middle of the nineteenth century, most magical work (like favourite recipes) was passed on by word of mouth within families and communities. A huge amount of knowledge must have been lost over the years. However, that does not mean that it cannot be recovered. Magic is nothing if not flexible, and we can each build up our own 'magical practice' concentrating on our own specific needs and talents. Even when we work with others we are still ultimately on a voyage of self-exploration.

For example, one of my daughters has always had a startling effect on street lights and traffic signals. When she passes certain street lights they shut down, and when she demands that a traffic light turns to green it does – often to the amazement of other motorists who weren't expecting it. Another daughter however has absolutely no effect on street lights, yet manages to make traffic lights stay green past their proper timing. She cannot make a light *turn* to green as her sister can, but she can certainly cause it to *remain* green. This is simply a combination of proper breathing, an iron will, plus constant repetition of 'Stay Green, stay green' as we approach. It may seem far-fetched, but it works for her and I've met a number of people who seem to possess the same talent.

Still on the subject of motoring, back in the days when I drove, I used to put a great deal of faith in an entity I call 'Our Lady of the Parking Space' Over the years she repeatedly found me parking spaces no matter where I was, which included central London on a couple of memorable occasions. How did this work? It wasn't as though I was the sort of person who could park on a sixpence. I *needed* help. And more often than not, I received it.

I believe this is where magic is often misunderstood. It's not always about saying the 'right' words or doing the 'right' rituals. The magical powers we develop often respond to our needs. If we regularly *need* a parking space, our inner or subconscious mind puts out feelers to find a way of solving the problem. This can include contacting appropriate powers or deities on our behalf. All we have to do is identify a need and ask our subconscious to find a way to help.

It goes without saying that if we want our subconscious to seek out things that will benefit us, we are going to have to make sure it's fit and healthy. An unhealthy subconscious is quite likely to seek out things we would be better off without. Think of it as a two way process: just as magic builds character, so our character builds the sort of magic we practice. If we try to run before we can walk, perhaps seduced by promises of riches, fame or other prizes it's easy to get into difficulties. This is one reason why magic has always been so closely guarded. Just as you wouldn't give a ten year old the keys to a Ferrari, so you don't give complex magical knowledge to someone who is just starting out. In both cases people end up hurting themselves or others.

So, where should we should we start? Most people have no tradition of their own to build upon and this can be daunting, like staring at a completely blank page and wondering what on earth to write on it. It's surprising – and sad - how many people buy beautiful, blank, purpose-made books for their magical work which they never actually use. And as time goes by, every blank page is a reproach, a reminder of their unfulfilled dreams.

In spite of their good intentions, people do often give up at this stage. They feel there's no-one to teach what they need to know. If there are indeed any great teachers out there they must have hidden themselves away in a mighty broom closet. Yet if we look closely enough most of the information we need is already within us, locked away in the inner or subconscious mind. All we need to get it working is a good helping of common sense.

When we were children we could access our inner mind without any problems. Our childlike world was glorious, we only had to think of something and it was so. Even if we had little money, our minds transformed everyday objects into amazing toys. Whenever the world could not supply something, our imaginations could make up the deficit. Cardboard boxes became pirate ships or racing cars, while beds became tents and castles. Lonely children even invented imaginary friends for themselves. Magic was natural to us then, simple and straightforward. Nothing was ever impossible.

And then what happened? When we grew older we let it all go. Worse, as we entered the 'grown up' world we learned to value material things as though they were the only true reality. And our real treasure, our magic, was not only lost but often flushed away down the nearest drain.

Well, now it's time to go on a quest to find and recover our childlike self. There are several ways of doing this. Obviously as an adult you are not going to be expected to leap into the nearest empty box and shout, 'Away me hearties!' while brandishing a cucumber sword. Besides, you'd probably feel so self conscious that you'd fall about laughing even if you were messing about in the privacy of your own home.

But hang on – laughing at yourself wouldn't be such a bad thing, would it? Do you do that any more? If you don't then it's high time you did. The magical world has a great sense of humour and there's nothing it likes more than cutting pompous would-be mages down to their proper size. Each of us possessed a rich vein of benign humour when we were children but forgot it as we grew up. Instead now we have satire, or sarcasm, where the joke is always at someone else's expense. We need to recover our childish sense of fun and yes, silliness. Magic *needs* fun.

You can have a wonderful time reclaiming your childhood imagination. Make blots of damp paint on a sheet of paper then fold it in half and press the edges down. Open it out and give it a title. The knack is to be spontaneous here. Don't take too long, just say whatever comes into your head. And as with learning to laugh at yourself, don't be afraid of humour. 'Cabbage and sellotape;' 'boots with kettle'; 'spaghetti and stiletto heels'. For the wonderful thing about our imagination is that the more we use it, the better, and more creative it becomes. Conversely, an imagination that is never permitted to stretch its wings will eventually shrivel and die of despair.

Now there are people who will try and insist that magic is such a serious, grand subject, you should never be frivolous about it. I think this is nonsense. If you come across any example of magic that strikes you as affected or pretentious you should immediately suspect the truth of it. There is nothing pompous about magic – although to be sure, I've come across some pompous practitioners of the magical arts over the years! Humour and magic are not mutually exclusive; in fact they co-exist very well together. And if you find humour lacking in certain magicians it's often a sure bet that much of what they teach is lacking in other respects too.

Here's a game you can try for yourself. Choose a simple word, for example, 'turnip,' and then insert it into well known sayings. So 'All the world's a stage' becomes 'All the world's a turnip,' or 'All the turnip's a stage.' And 'Fools rush in where angels fear to tread' becomes 'Turnips rush in where angels fear to tread,' or 'Fools rush in where turnips fear to tread.' And so on, for the possibilities are endless. 'A turnip in need is a friend indeed'… 'Turnips are thicker than water.'

It's surprising how many proverbs and sayings will become downright comical – but is this because it is a new way of seeing, or because there is inherent comical power in the word itself? Well, would you normally giggle about turnips? In the end you will find your chosen word takes on a life of its own. Just to think of it brings a smile to your lips because your game will have empowered it.

And magic is all about empowerment. Some words may well be powerful, because centuries of similar usage will have given it an underlying potency. However, this power only exists if you understand and add to its power. Within occult lodges suitable training may be given to initiates, but to the average person working only with a book such as this it's impossible. So forget Abracadabra and start creating your own magical words. And enjoy it!

Finding pictures in the clouds...

Another way of returning to childlike creativity is looking for pictures in the clouds. Most of us tried this when we were young. Ideally you would be lying in the grass, pleasantly sleepy, gazing up at a summer sky. Realistically you may be wet and shivering, sitting on a park bench or even looking at the sky through your bedroom window. It doesn't matter. The important thing is to *give it a try*. I've lost count of the number of people who have assured me they will tackle this or that magical exercise when they 'have the time' or when it becomes warm enough, cold enough or the planets are in a particular astrological alignment. This is prevarication, pure and simple. And prevarication is not only the thief of time, it is the death of magical practice.

You might reasonably ask at this point, what does looking up at the clouds have to do with magic? The answer is – a lot. What we are trying to do here is to recover our inborn facility to construct powerful visual images. You'll probably be surprised how much visual material is all around us. I can remember when I was young living in a house where a badly papered bathroom ceiling provided a mass of images: faces, animals, castles, landscapes. It was impossible to capture them in a photograph – all you saw was the wrinkled ceiling. Several times I tried to draw the images, but the moment I tried to get something down on paper, they vanished. When I looked back at the ceiling I couldn't find them again, no matter how hard I tried. These fleeting images of incredible beauty and detail were the product of a mere moment in time. And my magical imagination.

The following exercises are designed to enhance your visualising skills by working with clouds, leaves, walls etc. Start off in as relaxed a position as you can. Obviously if you are sitting on a bench in the rain on a March morning, this is going to be tricky, but do your best. Even in the worst conditions, *some* degree of relaxation is usually possible. Above all, don't be put off. After all, you aim to be able to perform magic in all seasons and not just in good weather. Ground and steady yourself before you begin, breathing in through the nose and out through the mouth to a count that seems comfortable for you. Steadying usually requires you to take twice as long on the out breath as the in breath. Once you feel calm and relaxed you can allow your breathing to find its own natural level.

Now start looking at the clouds. At this stage we are working only on what the clouds bring to us. Sometimes it can be really tricky to see anything other than a mass of grey or white. The thick, cotton wool texture of the *cumulus* clouds make them ideal for beginners, whereas the overall drab sheets of *stratus* clouds can be almost impossible at first. Don't let this put you off though. If you find nothing is happening begin by noticing the shapes of the clouds in their simplest sense, for example, triangles, squares or swirls. Sometimes these will trigger ideas and suggest pictures. Also you're more likely to see images if you think big. It's not uncommon for an image to be a hundred feet high (or more!) in a cloud picture.

If you're out cloud watching on a windy day remember that your pictures will be constantly on the move. Sometimes these alterations are plausible, for example a small animal may appear to grow into a larger one. At other times the changes are surreal, and a small animal may turn into a tree! Observing the changes is all part of re-educating your mind to understand the mercurial qualities of the imagination. In magic anything can – and does – happen!

Most of us can manage to observe the sky at some time during the week, and given the British climate it's fairly certain we will see plenty of clouds. However, you can find similar images almost anywhere, lurking in the bark of trees, the embers of a bonfire, puddles, concrete, leaves, kitchen towel, bars of soap... the list is endless. The more you practice, the more you'll notice. Magic is nothing if not obliging.

The aim of these exercises is to be able to look at any reasonable cloud and see something there. But of course this is observation, not magic. The magic begins when you start looking at the clouds and telling your subconscious *what you want to see*. Begin with grounding and the same initial breathing exercise to steady yourself, but instead of merely observing, try to create. Try saying to yourself 'I see a train' or 'show me a train.' Saying 'I want to see a train' is weaker, because who is to say we will get what we want? The precise wording and method has to be yours alone – what works for you may not work for anyone else. But you *must* be totally convinced of the reasonableness of your request.

How often do you hear people say things like, 'It's just my luck' when something unpleasant happens? Whenever something goes wrong in their lives, they talk as though it was to be expected, and was somehow 'due' to them. This is simply untrue. Bad luck is not prowling around, waiting to pounce on us. But if we act as though we expect bad luck then that is what we will get, because our state of mind will attract it. By a similar process if we expect our magic to work it will. But if we don't then we've doomed it to failure before we've lifted so much as a finger. Of course, you are going to have to work at this; a lifetime's negativity isn't going to be washed away simply because you say 'I feel lucky' once or twice. You have to completely change your mindset otherwise your subconscious mind *knows* that you don't really mean it.

Watching the clouds is a great way of increasing our confidence. First we see what the clouds bring to us. Then we tell them what we want to see. The purpose of the exercise is to learn to impose our will upon the visual processes and because it's relatively simple and straightforward it will bring results fairly quickly, which is very encouraging when you're just starting out.

The ancient Egyptians well understood the power of visual images. Their hieroglyphs did not only represent whole words, they contained *the essence* of the image itself. Indeed hieroglyphs were considered so powerful, especially in tombs, that some were defaced in order to stop them disturbing the repose of the Blessed Dead. Thus images of birds within a hieroglyphic inscription sometimes had their wings removed to prevent them flying around the tomb!

The Closed Eye
One of the most important sources of visual images is the closed eye. This is often neglected simply because we take it for granted we can see

only when our eyes are opened. Yet when we're half asleep, our eyes closed, we often see a whole gallery of images passing before us like a silent film. There seems to be something about the relaxed, near-sleep state that makes this possible. What happens is that we pick up images from the subconscious mind which is usually at its most just at the point when we're about to fall asleep. For many people this is a peak time for psychic activity and I've noticed that I've had some very strong premonitions around this time.

Conversely I've often managed to solve problems that have been bothering me for some time, just as I wake up. This is not only because I have moved from an unconscious to a conscious state but because my subconscious has been working on the problem all night, and has come up with a solution. Remember though that it doesn't usually work the other way (i.e. solving problems as we are moving from a conscious to an unconscious state, i.e. drifting off to sleep). In fact, if we dwell on problems as we're trying to go off to sleep all we tend to achieve is to keep ourselves awake all night!

You can help yourself to see these images by providing the best conditions for them. The reason we want to see them is because it's not only a way of working with the subconscious mind but it also sharpens up our visualising skills. So when you go to bed at night, settle yourself down and begin breathing to steady yourself. Don't close your eyes too tightly, and look up slightly beneath the eyelids. I've found this works best for me, but you might need to experiment a little to discover the best place to direct your unseeing gaze. You probably won't get images every single night, partly because sometimes you'll just drop off to sleep. Remember though, the more you show interest in your subconscious mind, the more it will show an interest in you!

On Circles and Magical Tools...

At first sight, Magic on the Breath probably seems laughably simple. You don't need to shut yourself away, chalk out a circle on the floor or gather together exotic ingredients, wands and athames. Unfortunately some people will try and make you feel that unless you set up a circle to cast your spell, it will lack power, or worse, backfire. Of course, there *are* times when casting a circle is appropriate and correct since it acts as a container for your power, and also deflects negativity or harmful forces while you are working. For example, if you are tackling ceremonial magic and summoning demons or discarnate entities into your Triangle of Art you really *must* cast a circle and keep within it.

However, the great strength of Magic on the Breath is that it can deal swiftly and effectively with everyday situations. It works because it harnesses your will and uses your breath as a vehicle to deliver the spell quickly where it is needed. This means you can do magic anywhere, at any time. Unless you feel strongly threatened, for example in situations relating to psychic self-defence, you don't need to cast a circle for everyday magic.

Keeping records of your spell work

A good spell caster can get by on nothing other than her bare hands, her will and her breath. However it's not realistic to expect to remember every single spell or exercise you perform. A hardback notebook is a good investment so you can write down the details of the spells you've cast and keep them safe (soft covers tend to disintegrate too quickly). You will need to jot down the details of how and when you cast your spell, plus the results and anything else that seems relevant, such as the time of day (some people find certain times of day better than others), moon phase or even your mood at the time.

Although there are people who claim they can remember everything, most of us need some notes, especially when it's for a spell you might need only occasionally. The advantage of writing things down, especially in the early days is that you can take time to 'get it right.' Also you won't waste time trying to remember what you did months or years before. Records also provide a valuable reference when you review your own spiritual growth at the end of each year. Magic is a lifetime's work – you'll be surprised how much your approach changes with experience!

If you use words or chants in your magic, you should record these too. With Magic on the Breath you don't need to use words unless you really find them helpful; your breath and will should carry the spell to its destination. I do understand though that many people feel no spell is complete without a chant or charm. Don't be misled into thinking that all have to rhyme; they don't, although setting a good rhythm for the words definitely helps with your breathing. What we must guard against however, is becoming so obsessed with rhyming that the intention behind the spell is lost or twisted.

Always try to record the breath pattern you used in your spell, e.g. breathe in for a count of three and out to a count of six. This will save you a lot of time later on if you need to perform a similar spell again. Sometimes breathing patterns do change, and you should make a note of this too if it happens to you.

Magical Tools
You can certainly do all the spell work in this book without any magical tools. I do however sometimes like to use a staff. This doesn't have to be anything fancy, even a pole from a sweeping brush will do. Please don't feel you have to go out and buy a special 'Magickal Staff' for this. Just improvise. I often use my walking stick. At a pinch you could even use a wooden mixing spoon and tap it on a table or worktop. The important thing is to understand the technique.

Staffs are particularly useful because they can drive a spell along the ground to its destination. Perhaps for this reason they're particularly good for spells involving animals. For example, a friend's neighbour kept allowing her dog to roam into other people's gardens. This dog would then dig, make a mess and behave quite aggressively. It wasn't the dog's fault; it was young and untrained and its owner should have repaired the fence to prevent it straying. So what should be done?

In this situation, we were faced with several options: to do a spell requiring the owner to repair the fence and prevent the dog from wandering (this was the best solution, but might take time to implement); to make the dog leave the garden and return to its own, (a more instant solution, useful until the fence was repaired) and to make it less aggressive generally, which would be a good thing in the long term.

In the end we decided to perform spells for the latter two options, while my friend got to know her new neighbour and could suggest fence repairs. This approach worked well especially since the dog was quite young and responded to simple magic. Tapping the ground gently with an old broom pole, and putting all the emphasis on a long straight stream of breath while breathing out, we sent the dog back to his own garden. The broom/staff drove the magic along the ground, and into contact with the dog.

I have sometimes had to improvise and use my walking stick as a magical staff to send animals in a certain direction, for example, away from a dangerous road or a river. Always use the exhaled breath to drive things away and the inhaled breath to attract them towards you. Don't be afraid to experiment; if you are dealing with a very heedless animal, you may need to hold the stick vertically and tap its end several times on the ground. This seems to carry the spell with more force, whereas other animals respond better if you hold your stick at a shallow angle to the ground and tap it gently. Remember that you are trying to work magic; you don't need to wave your stick about in a threatening manner and you certainly shouldn't hit anything with it other than the ground!

Linking the Staff to your heartbeat

A staff can be very effective if you link it to your own heartbeat. All that this means is that you tap out the same rhythm as your heart makes (something like *duh-duh, duh-duh*). Aim for something like 40 – 60 beats per minute. As you tap the ground, concentrate on your breathing, so you establish a regular pattern for your breathing, using your heartbeat to guide you. For example, breathe in to the count of four double beats of the staff, and then out to eight or whatever numbers you prefer.

In order to attract something magically, concentrate you intention on the inhaled breath. You can also draw your free hand (the one that isn't grasping your staff) to your heart as you breathe in, letting it drop to your side as you exhale. Conversely, in order to repel something you concentrate your intention on the exhaled breath. Your hand should then push the air away from you on the out breath before returning gently back to starting position – palm resting on the centre of your chest – on the in breath.

Important: *The biggest problem with magical tools is that we can become so focused on them that we forget about our will, our intention and our breathing. Without these, whatever else we may have, it isn't really magic.*

Breathing and Third Eye

For this exercise you will use the breathing and visualising skills you've learned so far in order to work with your 'Third Eye' which is located in the centre of your forehead, just your above your eyebrows. This can have many different names, including the brow chakra and it's existence is recognised by many different traditions and cultures. It is thought to be located deep in the pineal gland in the centre of the brain, and adepts are said to be able to open and close the Third Eye at will. Most of us however, pay it little attention which is a pity because even a little interest seems to go a long way. Doing this exercise is the equivalent to opening and closing this extra, psychic organ. You are, in effect, trying to wake it up.

Firstly ground yourself and take a breath to steady yourself. Then imagine you can actually *feel* your Third Eye. Take notice of what your real eyes feel like and project that sensation just above the bridge of your nose. When you blink as normal, imagine that the Third Eye blinks too. What it sees however is not the everyday world around you but the secret worlds, inner and outer, that surround us. It can see the future, it can see other entities. People who are clairvoyant or can see auras for example, are generally believed to have control over their Third Eye.

As you breathe in through the nose and out through the mouth as usual, you should visualise your breath also flowing in and out of your Third Eye. Choose a simple rhythm for your breathing and stick with it steadily. You don't need to do this for long. After a few minutes gradually slow down your breathing, finishing up with a long, soft, out breath, almost a sigh. As you do so, imagine the Third Eye closing again. It can help to actually shut your eyes while you do this. Wait a moment or two, and then take a few more steadying breaths before opening your eyes again. You only need to perform this exercise once or twice a week, don't overdo it. Over a period of time (most likely a few months) you'll notice it makes a huge difference to your magical work and you should become more aware of things that were once unknown to you. These could include increased psychic awareness, or the ability to see psychic gateways into other dimensions.

Things to think about before casting a spell

One thing all spells have in common is that they give shape to your intention. They make things happen. The problem is of course, that we have to be absolutely certain *exactly* what we're trying to do before we start. Woolly thinking has caused more bad spell crafting than just about anything else. If you doubt this then just eavesdrop on to the average conversation and hear phrases like 'What I meant was...' or 'She didn't understand...' Misunderstandings in everyday life are bad enough; in magic they can – and do - cause chaos.

The first thing you should consider is whether your spell is really necessary. Often problems can be solved without magic at all. Sometimes magical cleansing and dispersing negativity are all that is needed. Next decide whether to simply cast your spell or write it all down first. If you're a beginner, or it's a spell you've not tried before, it may take several attempts before you find the best way to say what you mean. That's another reason for taking a couple of steadying breaths before casting your spell - it's a last chance for you to reflect.

Important: *The written word is not the be-all-and-end-all of any spell. It only gives shape and form to the intention. If there's no force of will behind the spell then what you're writing is poetry. All the fancy wands and candles in the world won't be able to turn it into anything else.*

The best spells are usually the simplest. Don't worry about making words rhyme, just focus on your intention beginning with a single thought. Using our earlier example of trying to make a dog leave your garden, you could try 'Please leave my garden.' However, you don't want it running out into the street and causing an accident. So be precise. Say, 'Go back to your house' or 'Go back to your garden,' and since you don't want it to come bounding back again in the next five minutes, you need to add 'And stay there.' If you want to be really specific, try adding, 'Stay there until five o'clock'. Some dogs definitely seem to be able to tell the time. I have a St Bernard who always starts barking at our kitchen clock at 9pm because he wants his supper!

Once you've sorted out your precise intention, you need to use your breath as a catalyst to bind mind and will together. The breath then propels the intention off into the universe, a bit like firing a catapult. In this case we want the dog to go away, so you concentrate your intention as you exhale. (If we wanted him to come to us, we would have to concentrate when breathing in.)

Doing Magic for Personal Gain

In ancient times virtually all magic was concerned with personal gain of one sort or another. Most of the time there is nothing wrong with this; nobody would ever seriously suggest to a tennis player that winning Wimbledon would damage him spiritually. But you do have to use some common sense. The problem with excessive pursuit of personal gain is that it can blind us to wider issues, making us greedy, unfeeling and sometimes unscrupulous in the way we deal with others.

However, there are people who will try and tell you that you should *never* do magic for personal gain. I once met a practising witch (her own description, not mine) who held rigidly to this view, at the same time declaring that all magic for 'lofty aims' such as working for peace, saving endangered species, etc., was unworkable and doomed to failure. In addition she further hemmed herself and her followers around with all sorts of other ridiculous restrictions, until I found myself wondering whether she had ever actually cast a spell in her life. There's nothing wrong with not wanting to do magic; if that's how you feel then it's better to be honest with yourself.

But if you do want to do magic – read on!

Chapter Five
Thought Forms...

Descartes said 'I think, therefore I am.' Or more precisely, 'Je pense, donc je suis' often better known as 'Cogito ergo sum.' Practitioners of magic can take this a step further. 'I think, therefore I can produce a thought form.'

Although a surprisingly little known aspect of magical practice, thought forms exist in staggering numbers. In fact most people create several every day of their lives. Every single day. It's mind boggling. There are *millions* of thought forms out there. Most were created un-intentionally as we go about our daily lives, and last just a few minutes. Unless you're particularly sensitive you're unlikely to notice them. But they're out there, and they can affect us more than we realise.

Although thought forms are often used in hexing, they have many benign uses too including healing, guarding, protecting and psychic self defence. In order to use them effectively however, we have to understand how they can be created, both deliberately and unintentionally.

When we look in the mirror we see a reflection of our physical body. Surrounding that body, invisible to all but the clairvoyant are layers of colour. Think of it as a glowing outline all around us. We shall call this the auric field. I would like to be able to say 'This is what the auric field looks like' and leave it at that, but unfortunately not everyone can see it, and even those who can don't always agree what it looks like. Some believe it is made up of a rainbow-like spectrum of colours beginning with red nearest the body and violet furthest away. Some see *all* the colours simultaneously; others see them in succession and one of the best psychics I've ever known gets excellent results at reading just single colours. Others can't see them at all.

Luckily for our purposes we don't need to actually be able to see the auric field – though it helps if you accept that it exists. As I've said before, it's possible to be good at spell casting without being an expert on the mechanics of magic, just as it's possible to build a violin but be unable to play the instrument.

I was always taught to regard the human body as surrounded by layers of skins, rather like an onion. The first layer, the etheric body, lies directly on top of the physical body, and on top of the etheric body is the mental and then the emotional body. So there are four layers for us to remember: the physical, the etheric, the mental and the emotional bodies, in that order.

Between our physical body and the first layer, (the etheric body) there is a substance called 'First Matter' or ectoplasm. This is the strange gauzy looking material so beloved by Victorian mediums who seem to have generated yards of the stuff at séances. Ectoplasm is not a part of the etheric or the physical body, but a distinct substance in its own right and it has a unique property – it can be moulded by thought into different forms. Done properly, it can be made to resemble just about any living thing.

Because the etheric and physical bodies lie side by side, each influences the other even though they never quite merge together. It's this tiny gap or membrane between the two that allows the physical body to push the etheric one away from time to time. This is sometimes called projection of the etheric body. When this happens it can create something called the Etheric Double. Some of them can be very convincing while others seem to have been Photoshopped by a blindfolded donkey.

There are people who believe the Etheric Double is simply biding its time until it can cut the ties that bind it to its physical counterpart and become totally independent. Still others will assure you that etheric bodies have been known to attack and kill the physical body. Personally I take all these claims with a large pinch of salt. The etheric and physical bodies are interdependent, not rivals or enemies and you should never try to separate the two.

That said, there have been occasions when the Etheric Double has spontaneously separated from its physical counterpart at moments of great stress. During both World Wars there were many stories of soldiers who appeared to loved ones at the moment of death. It was as though the Etheric Double was making a last, desperate attempt to contact the people it had loved most on earth.

A thought form is rather different from the Etheric Double. Whenever we exercise our minds we create thoughts which are entities in their own right. They are created within the physical body before passing on out through our auric field towards the world beyond where they find themselves hunted by something called elemental essence. This lurks everywhere, unseen, unheard, pre-programmed to seek out discarded thoughts and give them some sort of physical existence. Now obviously, just throwing a thought at some elemental essence isn't going to make an *effective* thought form. To do this, you need to empower the thought with emotion. If you wanted to think of it as an equation, it would look something like this:

Thought + elemental essence + emotion = thought form

The more extreme the emotion the more vivid and sharply defined the thought form will be. And since destructive emotions tend to be stronger than pleasant, positive ones, it stands to reason that negative or frightening thought forms will be easiest to create and last longest. For most of us however, even thoughts generated by strong, negative emotions tend to be pretty short lived. Mostly we just create a thought, give it the necessary attention and forget about it. Sometimes we may return to it a few times, but we don't often concentrate on it very much. So usually thought forms have a fairly brief life span because when the thought and emotion are over and done with, the thought form just withers and dies.

At least, that's the theory. In practice some people don't always let go of their thoughts. Or perhaps the problem is ongoing, such as school bullying, family arguments, or long legal disputes. The same problem just keeps barging into our lives and won't let us ignore it. So what do we do? Usually, we feel better if we talk to friends or family and ask their advice. The old saying 'A problem shared is a problem halved' may be true for most things, but not thought forms. Before you know it you find the problem dominates your conversation and none of you can stop discussing it. It becomes, quite literally, a monster with energy building up and acting like a magnet for any elemental essence that happens to be in the vicinity. And then the thought form is here to stay, at least for a while.

It's surprising how far strong thoughts and emotions can travel although if there's nobody suitable nearby they may equally well turn around and return to you! It's particularly important to bear this in mind if you suspect your own auric field is already weakened. It's a bit like blood attracting all the sharks in the area.

Important: *Often when you've been practising magic for a short time you seem to hit a blank wall where nothing seems to go right. One possibility is that your auric field is attracting unwanted thought forms that then block your psychic activities. If you suspect this has happened to you, disperse any negativity and then psychically cleanse around yourself. You can even bless your bathwater by adapting the suggestions on page 40.*

I've gone into how thought forms are created in some detail here because we need to understand how they are created unintentionally in everyday life before we start trying to manipulate these forces and making them work for us. As with most things magical, thought forms are neither good nor bad *per se*, but reflect their creator's intention. A good intention creates a benevolent thought form. A cruel intention creates a little horror.

Generally speaking, like attracts like in the psychic world so someone who is insanely jealous will act as a magnet for pre-existing thought forms that originated with similarly jealous people. With each jealous thought, the person is feeding an ogre. Soon they find their problems have doubled and then trebled as they try to deal not only with their own problems, but with an ever hungry, ravenous thought form.

However, that's the down side. Creating thought forms can actually be very useful provided you know what you are about. It requires specific breathing patterns using inhaled and exhaled breaths of equal length, and you always breathe through the nose, instead of the mouth. This is in order to keep our intention close to us that fraction longer than it would if we breathed through the mouth. This will allow the breath to become more strongly imprinted with our thoughts and intentions. I usually count four seconds in and four out, although I have timed myself occasionally at five seconds. Whenever you feel strong emotions – delight, sorrow, anger etc., pay attention to your breathing. Strong emotions create clear thought forms. It's one thing to create a form deliberately, quite another to do so accidentally.

Once you understand how thought forms work you'll be able to get the best out of them. They have many uses, such as protecting others by weakening any negative forces around them. To do this we should find somewhere comfortable to sit, grounding and breathing to steady ourselves as usual. To create a proper intention we must concentrate on the person we want to help, visualising all the good things we would like them to have. But be precise and positive. If we want to keep them safe we imagine that *they are already safe*. We don't start thinking of them falling in the nearest canal and then saying to ourselves 'I don't want anything like that to happen'. Muddled thinking produces messy results!

Now think of your breath carrying your thoughts towards the person you wish to protect. Breathe out slowly, through slightly pursed lips, so that the air comes out in a long, shallow stream. Although the breath should be gentle enough not to disturb a candle flame, you have to give it shape; I always envisage my mouth forming a slightly flattened oval as I exhale. As you continue breathing, visualise protective thoughts reaching your target and gently attaching themselves to her like some sort of magical Velcro.

Of course, it's relatively easy if the person we wish to help has an auric field full of good, positive vibrations since beneficial healing thoughts will find it easy to attach and form a firm protective shield around her. If the target doesn't have good, positive vibrations however, it will be harder for the thoughts to anchor themselves because there will be nothing there to attract them. It seems very unfair I know, but it's actually easier to help someone with fewer problems.

When you create a thought form you basically brood upon it. You're not just sending out vaguely pleasant thoughts, you are sending them in a specific form, a form that you have chosen. Some people may send out an angel for healing, others could send a hobgoblin. It's entirely your choice. What must remain constant however is the amount of thought you give to it.

The thought form and the purpose for which it is intended must be constantly in your thoughts, so you must be consistent and learn to control extremes of emotion. I don't mean we should turn into hard, unfeeling automatons, but we shouldn't fall into the trap of turning every drama into a crisis either. Apart from accidentally creating unwanted thought forms, every extreme change in emotion can imprint itself on our auric field and leave a scar. Gradually our auric field gets used to these imprints of overwhelming emotion, and accepts them as the norm. This is one reason why bad habits are so difficult to break – our bodies don't actually view them as 'bad' at all! They have become conditioned to accept them as normal.

In creating your thought form it can help if you focus your thoughts on key words. These can set out its appearance, character and function. Sometimes a picture can also help. Eventually you'll begin to sense the thought form's presence as it connects with the elemental essence that surrounds us.

Just as no two thoughts are exactly the same, it follows that no two thought forms will be identical either. They are very difficult to reproduce exactly, although there are still people who firmly believe that if they recite the 'right' words, light the 'right' colour candle and wave a magic wand made of the 'right' type of wood, then they will get the same results every time. They won't. This is why it's so important to practice the breathing and visualising exercises in this book. They will help you acquire self knowledge in a way that isn't possible if you simply obtain all your knowledge from books (including this one). It's like driving on a stretch of road. No matter how familiar you are with it, every time you drive along that route you have to adjust your speed according to the weather conditions, the light, even the driving practices of other people who are out at the same time. No two journeys – or spells - will ever be identical.

So far we have looked at sending out protective thoughts with the intention of allowing them to attach themselves to the aura of the person you want to help. But there other types of spell that lend themselves to thought forms too. For example, love spells were extremely popular centuries ago, along with summoning up spirits to ask where Grandpa had hidden all his money! Supposing I wanted to create a thought form to make another person fall hopelessly, madly in love with me. Leaving aside the wisdom of doing such a thing, how would this actually work?

Let's take it stage by stage. First I would need to create a thought form full of passion and desire and then project it towards the object of my affections (for the purpose of this exercise we'll call him Bob). For it to have a hope of working, Bob needs to be capable of feeling love. If not, the thought form will find little to attach itself to, and may even continue looking until it finds someone more congenial. I could then find that Bob remains disinterested yet Fred, who lives a few streets away, is completely smitten.

Assuming however, that Bob *is* capable of love, and that the thought form attaches itself to him successfully, I would begin with grounding, take a few steadying breaths and focus my thoughts on love and desire, blowing them in a steady stream of breath away from me. To avoid missing Bob and accidentally targeting Fred, I would make sure I had something of Fred's to focus on, e.g. a photograph or piece of clothing.

I would keep up with this pattern of breathing and sending out thoughts of desire towards Bob in the hope that some of these would attach themselves to him and to the elemental essence in nearby, creating a thought form that would make him fall in love. *With me.* This last bit is important – and unfortunately it's often forgotten in the excitement of such spells. Instead what often happens – especially when you're just starting out – is that the thoughts we create do indeed reach our target. By now they may well have picked up some elemental essence along the way, and they do indeed arouse some passionate feelings in Bob. However this is *only in a general sense.* Yes, Bob's awareness of love may well be awakened. Yes, I may indeed cause him to fall in love – but that could be with someone else entirely!

Naturally if this happened I would regard my love spell as a dismal failure. However from a technical point of view it did work. I just wasn't careful enough when I crafted it.

People often find it difficult to know what type of thought form to create for a particular purpose. There is no 'one size fits all' in this work. For example, if you want to create a thought form to deter vandals from your property, it must be able to find something it can relate to in the auras of those people it will be dealing with. You cannot expect a gentle, reasoning thought form to have much effect on an axe wielding homicidal maniac. Likewise if you want to create a thought form to watch over a sick friend you should take care not to make it too scary! Driving away the demons of disease is one thing, terrifying the patient to within an inch of his life is quite another!

It goes without saying that you should never work with thought forms if you are tired or finding it hard to concentrate. This is because the emotions we use in creating the form can easily imprint themselves onto our auric field and this will attract more of the same in our direction. If you are too tired or absent minded to direct your form properly, there is a good chance it will rebound on you. An auric field is almost always initially damaged from within. Each of us possesses the means of our own defence – and the means of our own destruction.

Some people create thought forms as imaginary friends. Small children do it all the time, although they usually vanish in a year or so without any problems. While they exist however, these imaginary friends are as real as anyone the child knows at school and often much dearer to them. You should always allow children to find their own level in this and never initiate it for them. They will only create friends they are comfortable with and this in turn acts as a safety net for them, ensuring they don't get out of their depth.

As they reach their teenage years however, most children have given up on imaginary friends. This could be Nature's way of protecting them since the teenage years can be extremely volatile and thought forms produced during that time can often end up wreaking havoc. Teenagers go through such a gamut of emotions, driven by raging hormones they cannot control, that what starts out as a cheerful, friendly thought form can end up a ghastly tyrant. There is plenty of magic suitable for teenagers of all abilities, but in my opinion working with thought forms is not one of them. At least, not until their emotions have settled a bit.

One of the most popular uses for a thought form is to act as a guardian for your home or car. Ornaments – including garden gnomes or car mascots - can be used to represent these guardians and are useful as visual aids. As long as you give them regular attention they will remain active. One way of doing this is to greet them by name whenever you see them. The power of the name or *ren* was widely recognised in ancient Egypt and when people fell from favour their names were often removed from their monuments and tombs. The 'death' or destruction of the name was believed to cause the death of the individual in the afterlife. Conversely, if the name was preserved and spoken by future generations, this ensured a long and happy afterlife.

For guardian thought forms you must – as always - decide exactly what you want it to do. It is your servant – you are in charge. It can help if you make a list of what its duties should be. One problem is that it can be difficult to generate much emotion thinking about garden gnomes or guarding unless of course, you've had a recent burglary. The answer is to be more patient and persistent than usual. You need to think about the thought form as a real entity, something with appearance, substance and character. It should look just as you envisage it.

If ever you create a thought form that does *not* look as you planned, get rid of it quickly. Something has gone wrong and you have no idea of knowing what else may be different from your original plan. If you don't have a mascot or ornament handy on which to base your thought form, look for a suitable picture, something you can focus on several times a day. Ground yourself each time (in order to avoid projecting anything of yourself into the picture), and practice the breathing explained on page 60. Direct your thoughts onto and into the picture using a long, exhaled stream of breath.

Naming a thought form gives it individuality, a sort of psychic soul. An everyday name like 'Jack' is fine. I once knew someone who called the first thought form he created 'One' and the second one 'Two.' He was a little surprised when 'Two' began to manifest as two separate forms, and he found he had twice as much trouble controlling it. This was because every time he said its name he inadvertently visualised what 'two' meant. Needless to say he avoided calling his next creation 'Three.' You should also try and avoid irony when choosing a name since it has a nasty habit of backfiring.

Although thought forms are easily created and can make good and faithful servants, they can sometimes take on a life of their own especially if you don't pay proper attention to what you are doing during the early stages of creation. Years ago, at a time in my life when I had a great deal of worry, I created a thought form to be a supportive friend. Unfortunately, because I didn't really have my mind on what I was doing, the thought form grew stronger and became increasingly difficult to control. It wasn't rebellious, but it was intimidating. It was my own fault, and when I discovered claw marks on the bathroom door one morning I realised it had to go. Getting rid of an unsuitable thought form takes far more time and effort than creating it properly in the first place.

Having given your thought form a physical shape and name, think of the attributes you want it to have such as loyalty, energy and strength. However, it's no good stressing energy if all you want it to do is guard your car. In that case it would be better to stress watchfulness and steadfastness. A guardian thought form requires regular attention from you to keep it active and obedient. Otherwise it will either fade away or link up with other thought forms and assume a life of its own.

Next create a symbol that encapsulates everything the thought form represents to you. Some people look no further than a sign of the zodiac or a rune symbol, which is a pity because the more effort you put into creating this pictogram, the greater power it has. Make sure you keep it safe for as long as the thought form is active, then when it is over destroy the pictogram in fire and cast the ashes to the four winds (or running water). This symbolic pictogram can also be destroyed if the thought form shows signs of beginning to get out of hand.

It's even possible to create thought forms in cyberspace to protect websites. They may not fully protect against a determined hacker but can be very useful against what I call 'mindless mischief' and trolls. You need to have an area set aside online where you can regularly greet the thought form and invoke its protection every time you visit the site.

Thought forms don't last forever, but they can certainly last longer than intended. Many people claim that once you stop thinking about something it ceases to exist in the psychic world. This is a little optimistic. Normally they cease to exist once the originating thought has lost its energy. However if they have been picked up by someone else's mental energy, or if the originator of the thought keeps on generating more energy to fuel the thought form they can be very difficult to stop and sometimes do considerable harm.

Some people do seem to attract thought forms, probably because they are very emotional and their thoughts are just what the thought form requires. Even though it has long since detached itself from its original creator, it can still have enough energy left to propel it around the various psychic planes, looking for someone new to act as its docking station. Just make sure that someone isn't you!

Chapter Six
Practical Magic on the Breath

It's one thing to theorise about magic, but actually putting it into practice in our everyday life can be rather daunting. How and when should we use it? The choices seem endless. Some will use Magic on the Breath to try and defuse difficult or negative situations. Others will use it to 'blow' other people off sites like EBay just before the bidding closes!

What matters most is that you formulate your intention carefully. You can't expect your magic to sort out messy thinking for you! That's something you have to attend to yourself otherwise you can end up casting a spell and getting something you never, ever envisaged – or wanted. As in most things in my own magical practice, I tend to rely upon the old saying, 'As above so below,' which I mentioned back in Chapter One. You basically need to apply the same principles to magic as you do to ordinary life.

One of the great advantages of Magic on the Breath is that it is quick and simple. You can do it while driving, waiting for a bus or shopping. The possibilities are endless. You don't need special equipment, you don't even need to speak. However, any type of magic has the potential to leave you feeling tired and drained if you try to do too much too quickly. If you do feel tired, remember that's when you're most likely to make mistakes. Practicing the exercises in this book will help – magical fitness isn't unlike everyday physical fitness - but an exercise is an exercise and a spell is a spell. I've found one of the best ways to practice using real spells is to work with plants. You can experiment with driving away common pests such as greenfly or slugs, or attracting bees, butterflies and ladybirds. The usual principles still apply, concentrate on inhaling to attract and exhaling to repel.

Then you can move on to other small magical tasks that will help you put into practice what you've learned. People sometimes feel this is wrong that magic should only be reserved for really important work. I think that it's vital to try and hone our skills before we tackle bigger things. For example, you need to get someone to move. Perhaps they are part of a queue and taking too much time, or perhaps they're blocking your way and don't seem in a hurry to move. Obviously you don't leap in with magic – try offering to help the person in the queue with his packing, or just ask 'Excuse me please, may I pass?' of the person blocking your way. Nine times out of ten that will do the trick. If it doesn't then consider using magic, always remembering that there's a world of difference between giving someone a gentle nudge and a hefty shove!

Now of course some people will argue that this approach interferes with free will. It does, but so then does asking someone to move or forcing your way through a too-narrow gap! The easiest way to make this type of magic work is to harness the other person's wishes to your own. This can require some speculative guesswork on your part. You might put the thought into their head that they have an urgent appointment or something similar.

First ground yourself, take a few steadying breaths and then, while exhaling gently, begin mentally insisting, 'You don't want to be here. There's nothing here to interest you. You want to look at something else now...' or 'You should not stay here any longer, you have lots of other things to do...' As you are mentally sending out your intention, blow out gently through slightly pursed lips. You only want to nudge the person aside, not push him over.

I've heard it said that this type of magic is somehow dangerous. Maybe. In the wrong hands, with the wrong intention, *all* magic can cause misery. It can also bring great happiness. As I mentioned in Chapter Four, just as magic builds character, so our character builds the sort of magic we practice.

The same thing is true in everyday life. Some people only use their cars to go shopping while others use them to go ram-raiding. It's not the car's fault; it's caused by the character of the driver. If you're the sort of person who cannot go anywhere without getting into an argument or fracas then maybe magic really isn't for you at this stage.

One of the great advantages of Magic on the Breath is that after a while it becomes instinctive. You don't need tools (though you can use them if you wish) or spells, you just focus on your intention, harness it to your breath and either send it out or draw it towards you. You no longer need to weigh up the pros and cons or agonise over decisions. You know and understand what you will and will not do and you will discover that certain rhythms and breathing patterns will make the job easier.

As a general rule of thumb:
- If you want to attract something, concentrate on inhaling.
- If you want to repel something, concentrate on exhaling.
- Magic is most effective when you focus on the out breath.
- Sharp, short breaths bring about sudden, forceful change.
- A long, strong stream of breath is useful for dealing with stubborn, entrenched problems. It's particularly useful in psychic self-defence.
- A gentle breath should be used for magic intended to work on the sick, the young, the elderly or yourself. Remember when you wish to change something within yourself you need to be persistent but moderate.
- Persistent problems call for the longest breath you can manage.

When you get really experienced you can just 'instruct' when you cast spells. This is so simple that some people find it hard to believe it can work. But it does, and it's actually a very ancient technique, rather like the ancient Egyptian *ushtabi* figures. These were put in tombs as servants who would do all the work so that the owner could enjoy his afterlife. All the deceased had to say was '*Ushtabi*, do…'and then say what was required for example, '*Ushtabi* do the digging.' The *ushtabi* could only speak one phrase, 'I do, I do.' And yes, magic can really be as simple as that!

The Gentle Art of Writing your own Spells...
One of the wonderful things about Magic on the Breath is that you don't have to abandon any other magical methods that you already us and enjoy. You can easily add the technique to other things, such as written or spoken charms and it will empower them considerably.

Although I always say that a good spell-caster can get by with nothing but her bare hands, her will and her breath I recognise that many people like to recite written spells feeling their rituals aren't complete unless they have something to say, rather than something to think. Personally I believe that written spells are fine *provided you write them yourself.* I've never felt that a single spell can suit everyone and writing your own spells is simple once you get the hang of it.

Unfortunately over the years a certain mystique has grown up around this and people end up feeling that their own spells just aren't good enough. This is nonsense. What works for one person may not work for another who has different character, training or background. Writing your own spells has several advantages. They are unique to you, tailor-made for your precise needs and, because you've taken care choosing each and every word, they are already empowered with your own particular brand of magic.

However, you cannot write spells just by talking about them. The first few attempts will be difficult, but like most things, you will improve with practice. Wanting to write a spell is one thing, sitting down and doing it is quite another. The first spell is always hard to write, and the first line of the first spell can be an absolute nightmare. The blank paper seems to smirk at us and we're sorely tempted to screw it up into a ball and hurl it into the nearest corner. But restrain yourself, and set to work instead. Don't be put off, and don't leave it any longer – go and find a pencil and paper *now* and make a start.

For your first exercise I want you to choose a season or festival and write an invocation of no more than about four lines, asking for help to absorb the real lessons of this time into your life. The season or festival is entirely up to you. The word 'invoke' basically means to call up or call forth, so begin by thinking of whom or what you are addressing. If you don't feel comfortable with the idea of deities, invoke the spirit or force behind the season instead. In spring this could be growth, as plants burst into life after the long winter, so you might start off with something like, 'I call upon The One who wakes the seeds,' or 'After the dark and cold, may the Spirit of New Growth make me bright and warm.' If you get really stuck, make a list of all the things you associate with the season you've chosen. Write them down, close your eyes and run your finger over the list. The word you stop on will be your theme for the day.

Each season has its own characteristics, and some of these will 'speak' to you more clearly than others. For example, when I was a child I noticed that the winter night sky looked completely different around the Winter Solstice (21nd December). It had a strange, slightly greenish tinge, and the stars looked like diamonds on velvet. So for a Yule invocation you might begin with something like: 'Stars in the velvet dark of night...'

If you have a specific problem you want to solve with your spell during this season, you could try: 'This season I have come to ask...' Even if you don't end up using the line, it's important to get a few ideas down on paper.

Next think about what you'd like to achieve or learn in this season. It doesn't have to be a long list, a single thought is fine, provided it is something you *really* want or need. You can't bluff with spell writing; insincerity sticks out a mile. And remember that you are going to *say* your spell - you're not trying to write great literature. The simplest sentiments voiced from the heart work far stronger magic than fanciful poetry without an ounce of true feeling behind it.

Don't worry if by now you feel like throwing your pencil in the air and chewing the carpet instead. You should always allow yourself at least half an hour to 'get into' your spell writing. What's important is to put some ideas down on paper. I often doodle as well because it has a way of freeing up my subconscious mind. Trying jotting down a few key words and finding ways to link them together. If you've spent half an hour and still come up with nothing, go for a walk or make yourself a cup of tea and come back to it. Sometimes a change of activity is all that's needed to kick-start your ideas.

Once you've hit upon a line that you actually like, count the number of syllables in it. This means to count the number of actual sounds; 'dog' has one syllable, 'porridge' has two and 'catapult' has three. Although we're not trying to produce great literature, working with the rhythm of a spell makes a great difference to its power. If you can build up a good pulse the words literally roll off the tongue (or through the mind!). Not every line needs the same number of syllables, but there should be some sort of pattern, so for a four line invocation you could have any of the following patterns:

1. All the lines have the same number of syllables
2. The first two lines have the same number, the second two lines both have the same number as each other, but a different number of syllables from the first two. So you could have lines one and two with six syllables, and lines two and three with eight syllables.
3. Lines two and four have the same number of syllables as each other, and lines one and three share the same number. So you could have lines two and four with six syllables, and lines one and three with eight syllables.

The actual number of syllables doesn't really matter. Many people like to work with an even number, e.g. six, eight or ten. For some reason I often work with seven!

This is an invocation I wrote some years ago when I was struggling on my path and wanted help. I was in such a muddle I wasn't even sure what I needed to know, and in the end wrote an invocation to try and explain how I felt. There's nothing wrong in being uncertain! As a spell it worked too, because I spent so much time and effort working out what exactly I was trying to say. Eventually, as you can see, I explained my confusion, and the fact that I knew the answers were out there somewhere. Once the problem had been voiced the answers started coming in, as though I had set off a chain reaction somewhere. You will notice that lines one and three have seven syllables, whereas lines two and four have six.

You ask me for my questions,
The stars go spinning by
I wait upon your answers,
Goddess of Endless Sky.

You can see in this invocation I actually addressed my deity in the final line rather than the first. It just seemed to work better that way for me.

When you write something like this, don't be afraid to give it a trial run. Begin with a deep breath, and read the first line silently to yourself as you breathe out. Then breathe in again, and read the next line on the next out breath and so on. (If you breathe in as you read the lines you are preventing the intention from leaving your physical body and auric field.)

When you invoke someone or some power, you want to make every part of the spell reach them. Of course, when we speak aloud, most of us naturally do so in the lull between breathing in and out. So with a spell we have to say a line, and then breathe out while concentrating on sending the spell to its destination; then we take a breath, hold it, say the next line, and then breathe out again etc. It's not difficult, it just takes a little practice. I do understand that writing your own spells isn't easy, so if you are still stuck try using one of the following for the first line. I've included the syllable count to help you:

- *I look upon the northern sky (or western, eastern etc.) (8 syllables)*

- *Welcome Lord and Lady Bright.... (7 syllables)*

- *The stars hang frozen in the sky (8)*

- *Hunter of the Night, Lord of the Dark.... (9)*

- *I feel this time of year most keen (8)*

- *As the rain falls to earth... (6)*

I am often asked whether spells have to rhyme – they don't. However the care and attention we bestow on our written words does become an intrinsic part of the ritual. When we make a spell rhyme therefore, we imbue it with the quality of a chant, which can be very beautiful. The biggest risk is that we become so carried away with getting the rhyme right that we make a nonsense of the intention. One of the best ways of avoiding this is to invest in a good rhyming dictionary. As least then you have more choice of words!

When drafting your spell remain focussed on what you hope it will help you achieve. One day, sitting in a very muddy car park on a cold winter's day, I was thinking how much I was looking forward to the return of the sun in spring and summer. (For some unknown reason I did a lot of magic in very drab car parks at one time!) I felt I needed to write a spell to address the sun and invoke the warmth and optimism of the warmer seasons and come to terms with all the wintry cold and rain. So I began by writing 'Come back into my life once more.'

Then I thought that 'come back' sounded rather harsh and bossy, as though I was shouting at one of my dogs. So I changed it to 'return,' which produced my first line: 'Return into my life once more,' and still kept the original eight syllables.

The second line was going to be 'And warm the corners of my heart' until I realised that not only do hearts lack corners, but it was going to be fiendishly difficult to find a good rhyme for the word 'heart'. This is a good example of how easy it is to get carried away and throw common sense out of the window! So I changed it to: 'With life and love and honeyed flame.' I like honey, both as a food and a colour, it's warm and comforting and just what I need when I'm cold. Then I changed the first word of the line to 'bring' because I liked the idea of asking the invoked power to bring something to me. This gave me my opening two lines of eight syllables each:

Return into my life once more,
Bring life and love and honeyed flame.

The third line was not so difficult once I'd got the first two sorted. I first tried, *'Remind me of the days to come'* and then changed it to *'Reminding me of days to come,'* because this gave comfortable stresses on 'mind' and 'me' when I read it aloud. It's very important to keep trying the lines out as you work so that they sound natural and easy to recite. And of course this is continually empowering the spell, too.

The fourth line just flowed and didn't need alterations, because I already knew exactly what I wanted to ask. I'd addressed the solstice sun asking that he return not only to the earth but to me personally. So the finished invocation read:

Return into my life once more,
Bring life and love and honeyed flame,
Reminding me of days to come
And let me not despair again.

You will see that each of the lines has eight syllables, and even though it doesn't rhyme there is still a strong rhythm. I found that it worked particularly well when combined with soft, steady breathing. I also combined the spell with a libation of honey to the earth. Basically a libation is an offering (usually of oil, water, wine or honey) that is poured on the ground. I chose honey because I had mentioned it in the spell. I prefer clear, runny honey for libations, otherwise it just falls off the spoon in a great lump rather than drizzling gently. And a great lump of honey is nowhere near as nice to work with as the sort that trails in a thin golden ribbon!

It also easy to support candle spells with your breath and of course we worked with candles in some of the first exercises in this book. Candle magic has become increasingly popular over the last few years although they have been widely used in magic and prayer since the earliest times. We can use them to convey our entrusting spells and invocations to our chosen deities or just 'light a candle' for a particular intention. I often do this when people request healing or blessings, concentrating on giving the blessing on the exhaled breath just before I set the candle in its holder and light it. Here, a candle would be particularly apt for the winter solstice since its flame represents the promise of the returning sun. This keeps the intention of the spell alive for hours, although obviously you should never leave it unattended for safety's sake.

Some people like to charge their candles before use. This is very easy although some people do get the wrong end of the stick. At one of my workshops I was once asked whether it meant we had to run at our candles like a charging bull! The easiest way to charge the candle is by placing a *drop* of oil (scented, plain, or even olive or cooking oil) into the palm of your hand and gently stroke along the length of the candle from bottom to top. As you do this you can either talk about your intention (the subject of your spell) or even softly repeat the spell itself. You shouldn't just slap the oil on the candle and hope for the best. There must be a feeling that everything you use is specially chosen for the task in hand. Even small things have the right to feel important and useful! And they work better for you when they do.

When I was very young my father showed me that if you rubbed a nylon comb on your clothing or hair it would then pick up small pieces of tissue paper. Of course it wasn't magic, though when you're six years old it looks very like it! Charging a candle is very much the same - rubbing it attracts all those energies you send out in your magic. There is no inherent magic in a candle which is basically a lump of wax and string. As always, it's your intention and your will that empowers it. Simply lighting a candle and reading out someone else's spell will never be as effective as your own efforts.

Sometimes people argue that the colour of the candle we use is vital to the spell's success. I believe that our magical will can overcome any deficiencies in colour. And a plain white candle will work just as well as a coloured or perfumed one. I've used tea lights and ordinary household candles with just as much success as exotic coloured ones. Don't be tempted to re-use a candle though, since it cannot absorb more than one magical intention at the same time. You can of course re-light a candle if you are using it for the same intention as before.

You can also, if you wish, inscribe something the candle. It's not essential but can help to focus our intention. The writing itself – choosing the words, making your marks - is all a part of the spell and you should use your exhaled breath to will your intention into the candle. But don't overdo it. All you need is a word or two and/or a symbol. Distilling your thoughts into a single word is magic in its own right. So for the spell I have given here you could write something like 'Return' or even the Latin, *reverto nobis* (return to us). Always write the inscription before you charge the candle with oil - there's no point building up power in something only to then carve lumps out of it!

At all stages of treating the candle, whether you charge it, anoint it with oil or inscribe it, use your breathing to steady yourself and empower your intention. Even if you do none of these things, you should still breathe on the candle before you light it. The idea is to carry your will to the candle via your breath. When it is lit the candle will then carry your intention out into the world. Many people enjoy this kind of work because it makes more of a ritual out of a simple spell. But if you don't use a candle, don't worry, just return to your invocation as often as possible during the day.

Whenever we do anything with magical intent, we must imbue it with a sense of purpose. Don't simply go through the motions; make it special. You don't need to spend money, just invest each and every action with the sense of ritual. This comes from within, not from the tools you use. For example, when lighting candles, some claim you should never use anything other than a match because it is somehow more 'natural'. Yet years ago the same argument could probably have been used in favour of using tinder and flint as opposed to matches!

What matters is that you are *always* mindful of what you're doing. If this isn't possible, for example because others are present or you keep being interrupted then it's better to stop until you can give the task your full attention. That's the very least your spells deserve.

It's vitally important in all magic to only do what feels right to you. I remember being quite surprised when someone first told me that candles should always be extinguished with the fingers or a snuffer (which looks like a small dunce's cap on a stick). I've always felt that using the breath to extinguish a candle is a magical action in itself. And of course you can turn it into a ritual in its own right. I hold out my hands, palms facing each other, about eight inches apart, either side of the candle flame. I then take a deep breath, pushing my ribs out as I breathe in, pause, then exhale out firmly, pulling my stomach muscles in sharply as I do so. This expels the air in a long, steady stream, while

I visualise the smoke from the candle flame carrying my intentions (e.g. healing or loving thoughts) towards the intended recipient.

Although making a ritual is a wonderful aspect of magic, don't let it drag. If you keep everything swift – but not hurried - and decisive, you will use it often; long spells tend to get shut away in dusty books! Even on the busiest day, you can find a moment or two to mentally read or recite aloud whatever you've written, and you can return to it again throughout the day whenever you have time.

The effort of creating your own spells is repaid a thousand-fold in the results. You don't need a lot of extra ritual because so much work has already been done - choosing gestures, breathing patterns, words or symbols - during the creation of the spell. Using a ready-made spell means you have to work that much harder to empower it because it is simply words on a page with no real connection to you. This is why spell books often give you lists of other things you need, because the effort of gathering them together is almost the only way of involving you directly in the spell.

Chapter Seven

Hidden Magic and Magical Harnessing...

Nowadays it's not that difficult to find a variety of books on almost any aspect of witchcraft, the occult or magic that takes your fancy. Even if you don't like the idea of your family or neighbours knowing about your interests, you can always browse the internet. Centuries ago however, any interest in magic beyond the occasional folk charm had to remain hidden. If you lost your temper and muttered a few angry words under your breath you had to hope your neighbours' children or cows didn't suddenly sicken or you could find yourself the prime suspect in a witchcraft trial.

Many of these accusations seem laughable nowadays, except for the fact that so many ended in the death of the accused. Even those Cunning Men and Wise Women who offered charms *against* witches and sorcery could all too often find themselves on the wrong side of the law. Their neighbours could consult them about reversing hexes one day, and accuse them of witchcraft the next.

Given the dangers, it's surprising magic survived at all. Yet obviously it did, and magical traditions persisted, from reading tea leaves and charming warts to other, more complex ideas. It suggests that a great deal of magic not only worked, but that it must have been possible to perform it discreetly. Instead of using special tools set aside only for magical purposes, people must have used everyday items in such a way that nobody noticed what they were doing. Those who were never accused, and lived to pass their skills on to the next generation must have kept very quiet about it. Indeed, both occult and arcane mean 'hidden.'

The strong link between breathing and magic was certainly suspected however, as the old idea of 'scoring a witch above the breath' occurs in many accounts of witch trials. The idea was that if you made a suspected witch bleed somewhere above the nose and mouth, you could break the power of her spell.

Before the 1870 Education Act, most children never had a chance to go to school. Even if they could read a little, most didn't learn to write. So the idea that *every* Wise Woman and Cunning Man kept their own Book of Shadows' is rather unlikely. Most skills were passed on orally rather like household hints and recipes. Some families had their own specialities, such as healing, working with animals or weather magic.

With my own family their area of expertise was hexing. I left their tradition fairly early on in my life, long before I had really been trusted to learn all their secrets. I do know though that whenever I asked outright if they believed magic existed they would deny it until they were blue in the face, and if the conversation ever wandered onto the topic of witches, magic or the supernatural they'd quickly change the subject. 'Just old wives' tales,' they'd smile. 'Don't worry about it.'

And this of course, is one of the biggest differences between then and now. People are much more willing to talk about magic, paganism, witchcraft and all sorts of beliefs and practices. In those days people would deny it until their dying day. It wasn't the sort of thing you could have a real conversation about, at least not when you were young. The flow of information was so strictly controlled it surprising anyone learned anything at all. So how did it work in practice?

From my own experiences, many years ago, I know you had to show just enough interest. Not too much though. Too many questions, too quick a temper, the suspicion that you might not use your gifts in the way the family approved of, all these things could cause the lessons to stop. Forever. So you had to get the balance right. Then perhaps one day someone would make a comment that wasn't quite what it seemed. If you picked up on it quickly enough you might be told a little more. But these were only small snippets, just testing to see what you did next.

If you acted on the advice you were given and it was clear you were interested you would receive just enough information to help you build up a particular skill. It was a long, slow and frustrating process. Yet it was also understandable. The Witchcraft Act was never full repealed until the early 1950's, and some of us have always suspected that given the right conditions such intolerance could easily return again.

Of course, it's not only witches or magicians who cast spells. People of all faiths (and none) have cast them at one time or another, although many would never dream of admitting to it. Also not all pagans practice magic. For some it never forms part of their spiritual life while others practice it rarely. One of the most unpleasant spell casters I ever met was certainly not a pagan and went to Church every week, regular as clockwork. Although she regarded herself as a pillar of the community, her magical work was, without exception, spiteful and malicious.

Doing Magic on the Breath is so very simple once you try it that you wonder it has been overlooked for so long. I believe one reason is that it deliberately hid magic from general view. It was safer that way. After all, if you were spotted late at night gathering mandrake, henbane or other magical herbs it would be difficult to come up with a convincing excuse. However Magic on the Breath, particularly when combined with simple everyday tasks, could easily be passed off as housework. Unless you charged outsiders for your services or bragged about your magical talents, nobody was likely to guess what you were doing.

Indeed, the boring and repetitive nature of many household tasks actually lends itself well to spell work. The quiet, inoffensive woman sitting in the corner, rocking her baby's cradle or busy with her needlework could well have been occupying her *mind* with completely different matters. Mind you, I have to say that we didn't actually have any quiet, inoffensive women in my family!

People still often believe that magic is all about waving a wand, chanting, making potions and casting circles. Actually some of the most effective spell work makes use of the physical effort involved in mundane tasks such as washing dishes or even clothes (if you do them by hand). These are particularly good for purification magic. You simply transfer the physical effort you put into the washing to the magical undertaking you have in mind. I call this Magical Harnessing.

Since these are fairly energetic tasks, I find that simply breathing in through the nose and out through the mouth works best. Don't forget we are all only human. There will be times when your breathing patterns will be interrupted, perhaps by conversation but you shouldn't let this upset you. Magic is very adaptable and can easily be made to fit around most things.

There were – and still are - a wide variety of tasks suitable for adapting to spell work. Apart from everyday chores such as baking, sweeping, and washing, there were crafts such as sewing, knitting, spinning, weaving, and quilting. Nor were such crafts restricted to women only, for in some parts of Britain knitting was regarded as a men-only occupation! Even just sixty years ago most women learned how to knit out of necessity in order to clothe their families. Yet knitting can also be a clever means of disguising magic since each stitch must be created individually, giving ample scope for strong and complex spell work.

In some communities there was a tradition that every pattern had a hidden message or blessing within it. This was particularly the case with Aran knitting. Admittedly this is highly skilled, but even a simple pair of plain bootees follows the same principle: every stitch or row can be bound into the spell for the child's health, strength and protection. For a house blessing you could knit a pot holder or even a string dishcloth!

The important thing with this type of magic is to pick a task in keeping with your own practical skills. If you're a novice knitter stick to a simple square – the magic will still work. It's the method, not the knitted end product that counts. Keep your breathing relaxed and gentle for this, because it's a very time consuming spell. The aim is to combine the work (knitting) with your intention (subject of the spell) and your breathing just as you would for ordinary knitting.

A simple rhythm of breathing both in and out through the nose would be perfectly adequate as it helps focus the magic as close to the knitting as possible. Also, it's much more relaxed and natural, the way most of us would breathe anyway. Remember though there is a big difference between keeping the mouth closed but relaxed and keeping it tightly shut so that your lips form a single straight line! If you are tense it will affect your magic – think of it as wearing a tight collar while running a marathon.

It also helps if you sometimes pause and 'breathe' on the work in hand. This helps to fix the spell or blessing and concentrate its power. It also prevents your mind from wandering too much. There's no hard and fast rule about when or even how to do this, practice is going to be your best teacher. You could hold the piece of knitting up as though reviewing it for dropped stitches, and breathe out *through the mouth* so that you're actually breathing on the work while mentally focussing on your intention. For example, you might mentally state, 'May baby (*Name*) have good health and long life'.

Specific stitches are particularly good for certain intentions. Stocking stitch (with one row plain and the other purl) is good for smoothing out difficulties since it produces a simple smooth surface on the 'right' side. Ribbed stitches (e.g. one plain, one purl) are useful for situations where we need to hold on, or find ways of resolving differences. Garter stitch (every row knitted plain) helps remind us to stay grounded and can also act as an offer of help to others.

Knitting has its own unique rhythm, no matter whether you're an experienced knitter or a complete beginner. Just remember to keep up the rhythm and mentally repeat your intention regularly as you work. Each stitch and row will then build up slowly into a mesh of power. Some people also bless and empower their needles and wool each time they sit down to knit. Again you can simply breathe on them (a warm breathe, through the mouth) and mentally order them to become powerful transmitters of your intended spell.

If you're an experienced knitter you might like to knit a garment for the recipient of your spell. Even a scarf or a bobble hat is quite suitable. If you cannot manage this however, just start off with magic squares. These are three rows of three stitches each, seven rows of seven stitches or nine rows of nine. In such a small project it is quite easy to empower every single stitch with a magical intention. Apart from being quick to make, if secrecy is essential in your magical work you can always claim to be working a tension or pattern sample!

Embroidery is another useful way of fixing your spells, this time into cloth. Again your work can be as complex or as plain as you like, and the choice of pattern is entirely yours. For example, you might use a traditional symbol, such as a heart for a love spell. Or you could embroider something more naturalistic, such as a flower. All your emotion and desire can be worked into the stitches, so that the finished work becomes a tangible part of the spell. Since projects can often take several days or even weeks, you can bless and empower your fabric and threads each time you settle down to sew. As with any craft, if you're a complete beginner there are usually plenty of books in the library that will teach you the stitches.

Using Magic on the Breath when embroidering employs the same basic techniques as you used for knitting. Again, certain stitches lend themselves to particular types of spell. Satin stitch and blanket stitch both work well on love spells. Chain stitch and French knots are good for binding work, since you are making individual knots with each stitch. They can easily be disguised as flower stamens and pollen. Regular work on your embroidery or knitting gives you a chance to build up a tremendous body of power in each piece.

Whether you've chosen to embroider or knit, remember at the end of each session to spend a little extra time breathing your intention onto your work. Exhale gently through the mouth onto the item you're working on, using your will to carry your intention towards its target. If anyone happens to notice, you could always claim to be breathing a sigh of relief after so much hard work!

If knitting and embroidery don't appeal then try drawing and colouring your chosen symbol. Even if you are a complete beginner, you could trace a picture from a book or magazine, and spend some time colouring or painting it. It's always pleasant if you end up with a work of art at the end of your spell casting, but it's not vital to the success of your magical work. Actually the process of colouring is immensely therapeutic, as anyone who's ever used a child's colouring book will tell you. Again apply the same principles of breathing while working, breathing *on* the work and focussing your intentions.

Sweeping the floor is a wonderful exercise for banishing negativity and I think it's one of the most useful skills we can have. Negativity can accumulate virtually anywhere and for a wide variety of reasons. It attaches itself both to people and places and once it gets a hold it sits there, stifling normal thought and emotions, colouring them all with its own inky hue.

Of all the things I am ever asked to help with, banishing negativity is the one problem that recurs most often. You can adapt the exercise for banishing negativity in Exercise 4, Chapter Three (page 35) to make it appear that you're simply sweeping the floor. It's unlikely anyone will notice that instead of sweeping back and forth you are in fact sweeping in a figure of eight shape. If you find this difficult, try chalking the figure eight on the floor, a thorough brushing should erase it afterwards! Don't make it too large, about a metre/yard long is fine so that you can sweep from top to bottom in a single stroke.

When I was young we always swept carpets to clean them; the vacuum cleaner being considered far too rough and destructive for daily use. Mats were hung on a line and beaten clean to get the dust out of them; another process that can easily be adapted for banishing negativity without anyone being any the wiser!

As you sweep nobody is likely to notice your breathing, it will just seem as though you are really putting some effort into it! Remember when you are blowing negativity away you aim to produce a long firm stream of air, pursing your mouth just as you do when you are about to whistle. In fact, whistling has long been an integral part of magic, people used to believe you could 'whistle up a storm' while at sea. This is why it was considered so unlucky to whistle on board ship. Miners believed that someone whistling underground could cause an explosion and actors traditionally refuse to allow anyone to whistle in their dressing rooms.

There is old saying, 'Whistling women and crowing hen are neither use to God nor men.' Women who whistled were believed to conjure up the devil. To me this suggests that whistling – which is underpinned by the breath - had a strong magical application back in the distant past. Of course whistling is nowhere near as common now as it used to be although it can still be used especially when working with windy weather.

Most people begin learning to whistle on the inhaled breath and then progress to whistling on the exhaled breath. Actually it's possible to do both without stopping for a breath. The easiest way is to whistle a different note as you change direction with your breathing. However it's much harder to control the rhythm and counting. Since everyone seems to use a different method for whistling (when I was younger I could whistle in my throat!) you will need to experiment for yourself. However, realising that such things are possible is often half the battle.

Household tasks have an almost endless application for magic. For example, nowadays when we iron we simply plug an electric iron into the socket it's easy to forget how different things were years ago. Then you had to use the four elements: fire (to heat the irons), water (the clothes had to be damp), air (steam from the hot iron on damp linen) and earth (usually people did their ironing on a pile of old woollen blankets on the table). It could be heavy work since some of the larger irons easily weighed several pounds and it was very time consuming.

However, it was ideal for Magical Harnessing and also incorporated the four elements (fire, air, earth and water) without anyone noticing. You can adapt this to the modern iron quite easily, and at the same time say a little blessing for your female ancestors who struggled so hard to iron the heavy clothes. Magic using an iron is good for when you are trying to smooth out difficulties or solve problems.

Working with the Elements...

When working with the four elements of earth, fire, air and water, you need to understand how they affect us in everyday life. The Earth is traditionally associated with the north, and with our five senses of sight, hearing, touch, taste and smell. It governs the way things are in the present and how they were in the past, and can reveal the hidden properties of natural items such as herbs, crystals etc. Water is associated with the west and the emotions. It is susceptible to outside influences, and can attract psychic phenomena.

Just as it conducts electricity, so it also conducts etheric influences. It is closely associated with healing, discovering the true nature of the world (and people around us). Air is associated with east and with the intellect. It will govern anything requiring logic or rational thought. Finally, fire is associated with the south, and is connected with intuition, discovering meanings and unravelling the true nature of certain relationships. Unlike earth which is concerned with the past and present, fire can assist us with the future. It traditionally governs the realm of the imagination.

My favourite method of using the four elements in household magic is to do a bread making spell. Bread belongs to an ancient and honourable tradition, forming a staple part of many diets. Most countries have some form of bread whether it's made of wheat, cornmeal, rye, barley, oats or other cereal.

Some years ago the body of a man preserved in the peat was found at Lindow Moss. He had been sacrificed around the time the Romans invaded Britain. When the contents of his stomach were examined it was found he had eaten a portion of blackened barley bread not long before he was killed. This seems to suggest that potential sacrificial victims had drawn lots by each taking a portion of the bread, and the one with the blackened piece was the 'devoted one' or sacrificial victim.

Bread was an important part of the ancient diet since it is rich in carbohydrates. This is something we try and avoid nowadays but it was very important back in the days when most work was physically demanding. Indeed bread was considered such a vital commodity that people have been casting spells to ensure a good harvest since earliest times, sometimes making sacrifices in the cornfields to ensure fertility in the following year.

Nowadays we take our trips to the supermarket for granted, but years ago there were no convenience foods, and you had to prepare and cook all your own meals. Bread making *is* time consuming (it can easily take at least two hours from start to finished loaf) and hard physical work, although the end product is far superior to the flabby stuff that often passes for bread nowadays. If you use Magic on the Breath in combination with bread making, you are harnessing your magical intention to the effort of making bread. To me the process of 'proving' the dough until it doubles in size has always been pure magic. Bread making – like making jam – seems to bring out the alchemist in us.

Making bread has a lot in common with casting a spell. The secret of making a good loaf of bread lies in the effort you put into kneading the dough. The secret of casting a successful spell is the effort you put into the visualisation. Kneading dough requires force, patience and effort – and so does magic.

At its most basic, bread contains just five ingredients: flour, sugar, water, yeast and salt. Flour and sugar come from plants, grown in the earth, nurtured by air, sunshine (fire) and rain, and all four elements are present within. Salt represents either water or earth, depending on whether you use rock or sea salt. Water is one of the elements, and yeast being a living organism is linked to both the earth and the air.

Although yeast looks dead and dry if you're using it dried (otherwise it looks like a lump of putty) once it has a warm temperature (fire), moisture (water) and sugar (earth) to feed upon, it comes alive. Then it effervesces and produces carbon dioxide, (air) and small amounts of ethanol alcohol. This, added to the flour with more warmth and water makes the dough rise and double in size. The extra heat required to cook the loaf kills the yeast so that it stops rising.

As you can see, making bread uses the four elements over and over so they are all present within the finished loaf. Furthermore, the bread will go through a triple state of being, from the raw ingredients through the risen dough and finally, after a period in a hot dark oven it is reborn as a golden fragrant loaf. It pays to keep all these images in mind when working your magic. To complete this magical floury pentagram all that is required is 'spirit' which you will supply in the form of your magical intention and power.

Using Magic on the Breath, you will need to work in several stages. You could begin by grounding yourself as you collect together your ingredients. Then as you start mixing them you need to establish a comfortable breathing pattern. For the energetic process of kneading (for which you should allow at least ten minutes and preferably longer) your breathing will naturally change. Don't fight this, go with the flow. Give a little more force as you exhale and focus on your intention.

You can add to this spell in many different ways. I often call upon the spirits of each of the four compass points. Starting with the spirits of the North, guardians of the earth, I would thank them for the gift of flour and sugar, and ask their blessing on my spell. At this point it's important to mentally state what your magical intention is – often we become so engrossed in kneading the dough that we forget! You can also link what happened during the process of growing the wheat or sugar to your intention. So you could say something like, 'Just as this wheat/sugar cane/sugar beet grew in the earth, so may [Name] grow in health/strength/wisdom' (or whatever your intention happens to be).

It also helps if you can actually turn and face the correct direction but for most of us, working on a kitchen worktop, this will be impossible. You can however place at least some of your ingredients in the correct position, a bag of sugar to the north, a box of matches to the south, a jug to the west and the packet of yeast to the east. You can then face the correct direction mentally, even if physically you don't really move.

When you address the spirits of the East, guardians of the Air, you refer to the air in the dough and the air that separates the wheat from the chaff when threshing. 'As this dough will grow in size, so may [Name] grow in health/strength/wisdom etc.' Remember that everything can be said mentally if you prefer.

Address the spirits of the South as the guardians of fire. Then refer to the warmth that makes the wheat, yeast and sugar grow. When turning to the South, you can say, 'Guardians of the South, Blessed Spirits of Fire, you send the warmth that makes the wheat grow and the dough rise. As this dough will grow in size, so may [Name] grow in health/strength/wisdom etc.'

Finally turn to the spirits of the West, guardians of water, thanking them for sending the water you used to mix the dough, and the rain that made the wheat grow. 'Wash away [Name]'s ill health and make him/her strong again.' Each time you address the spirits of the compass points remember to breathe gently upon the mixture to carry your intention into the dough. There are long periods in bread making when nothing much will seem to be happening, but don't worry about this. We may forget about magic but it rarely forgets about us.

You may wish to use your breath again as you shape the dough into loaves. It doesn't matter from a magical point of view whether you bake them in loaf tins or on a flat tray. Some people swear by plaited loaves if the subject of the spell is female although this is really a matter of choice. Just hold your hands with the palms facing each other and your fingers pointing upwards over each loaf. Then breathe out gently as you express your intention once more. And when you finally place your loaves in the hot oven, commend your efforts to your higher powers or deity, repeating your intention and asking them to purify and bless the loaf with fire. This can be as simple as saying 'Be blessed, be cleansed, etc., and may fire purify and strengthen this intention.'

If you make bread in a bread making machine, you can still adapt this magical method although obviously there's less physical effort to be harnessed. Instead you'll need to concentrate on casting your spell while you are actually adding the ingredients to the bread maker bucket. However there's no reason why you cannot still invoke the compass points as above. When the machine is about to bake (usually about forty-five minutes before the end of the cycle) you can still request that the loaf be blessed and purified in the fire.

When the loaf is baked and cool, you are perfectly free to eat it just as you would any other loaf. Of course, it's quite possible to do a spell to make the bread sacred, perhaps to include it as part of some other ritual. Otherwise the loaf is only the vehicle for your spell; it is no more sacred than your sweeping brush or a darning needle!

Chapter Eight
Empowering your spells...

Many people say they find it difficult to put enough 'oomph!' into their spell. All the magic they see in films and on television is spectacular looking stuff, not just standing around breathing on things. Of course it's easy to forget that on television the 'magic' happens due to a team of special effects crew who work hard so you can 'see' the impossible. With my methods you do get results, *but only if you actually do the work*. If you just sit around reading or thinking about magic, you miss the point. Magic has to be practised. The more you practise, the better you get.

I once spent quite a lot of time trying to help a friend who was convinced she was under psychic attack. I wrote down precisely what needed to be done and how to go about it. We talked it through several times. A few weeks later, she was still complaining of problems and told me the spell was useless. It was only when I asked her point blank that she admitted never doing the spell or the exercises because she was 'too busy'. Just as medicine doesn't work if you don't take it, so spells can't work if you don't actually perform them.

Magic on the breath is a form of operational magic where all the power comes from within, and therefore can be virtually undetectable. This doesn't mean it has no power, although it can certainly be difficult to see or quantify. Sometimes people believe that sending a spell into the cosmos is just like pulling on a catapult. The more stress you apply the further it will go. But actually less is often more in magic. It's like trying to use a sledgehammer to open a window. If you apply inappropriate stress to a spell you risk destroying it altogether. However you will hear so much about empowering spells through sacrifice, blood and sex that it's as well to look briefly at them here.

Sometimes people try to tell you that in order to perform effective magic, spells must have a climax either using sacrifice or blood-letting in order to 'set the spell free'. Unfortunately this is often used as an excuse for cruelty. My own view – and I feel this very strongly – is that it is *our* choice to cast a spell and we have no business making anyone or anything else pay a price in pain for that. Even if a third party tells you they don't mind and are willing to experience pain on behalf of your spell, you should still question whether you're entitled to inflict it. If you did, you'd not only harm a third party, you'd also harm yourself. Cruelty is curiously addictive. Yet it won't make your spell stronger; it might even destroy it completely. It's much easier and more effective to harness your breath to carry your spell to its destination and put some real effort into that instead.

Another popular misconception is that alcohol or drugs are essential in order to empower a spell. Again this is something that easily gets out of hand and abused. While I can understand that both drugs and alcohol may make the person casting the spell less inhibited, they can also make him reckless. An uncontrolled spell will not necessarily do what you intend, and may miss its target altogether, something I've seen happen rather too often. Again there is the problem of addiction which is something that must be avoided if you want your magic to be reliable.

My own feelings are that although I enjoy a nice meal accompanied by a glass of wine or cider, I would rather avoid them when doing magic. Besides, there are times when you need to do a spell but it's neither appropriate nor possible to drink or take drugs. I've certainly never found my magic suffered because of it.

Sexual climax is also popular for empowering spells. It *can* be very effective and unlike sacrifice there are rarely any ethical issues to be overcome provided those involved are consenting adults. Sex does involve distinctive breathing patterns, although these need to be controlled for magical purposes, which isn't always easy.

Also, using sex to empower a spell relies heavily on visualising the intended result, and not many people, if they are honest, will reach a sexual climax while visualising healing a third person. Most people find it easier to visualise the magical intention immediately after the climax. Unfortunately there is a tendency to visualise all sorts of things just before the climax, which can weaken or subvert the spell anyway.

Another problem with using sex to empower a spell is the risk that because it is (hopefully) enjoyable, some people will cast spells simply in order to have sex. When this happens, the original magical intention becomes so lost and distorted that you may as well not bother. So yes, you can use sex as part of your magic, but to use it well is not as easy as some people would have you believe.

Using the Weather...

If you really feel your magic isn't going to be complete without some added empowerment, then I'd recommend using the weather. Mention the phrase 'weather spell' and most people think of dancing in a circle to make it rain or trying to raise a storm. It's quite true that years ago, food was always produced locally, the weather was vital in ensuring the success or failure of the harvests. If it failed the community would starve. Too much sun and nothing had chance to grow in the scorched earth. Too much rain and the crops went rotten in the fields. Children were told not to splash water with sticks at harvest time to ensure the weather remained fine, while whistling was believed to conjure up storms. Obviously anyone who seemed to be able to influence the weather would be both highly feared and in great demand.

However, that's not the sort of weather spell I have in mind here. Instead I want to show you how to harness the existing weather conditions to reinforce the imagery and help empower your spells. Extreme weather such as storms, high winds and rain are particularly useful. Given that weather can be so variable, even in the same month, working with it can add a whole new dimension to your magic!

Keep your spell intention short and simple, repeating it several times and each time ending with a long, firm, exhaled breath to carry your spell *into* the weather. Aim to build up a good, driving rhythm. Obviously it's easier if you work outside - there's nothing quite like casting a spell out in a storm! -but in extreme weather conditions that isn't always such a wise idea. It's important though to visualise your breath streaming away from you towards the elements.

One way of doing this is to link weather to your spell intention and your breathing. For example, if you're doing a spell for someone in pain, you could link this to the rain, as in, 'Just as the rain is falling now, so [Name's] tears are falling now. But when the rain stops, may [Name's] pain be gone.' Here you link the rain to tears caused by pain, though it could just as easily work with other causes such as grief or anger. This is a very old method known as 'like curing like' or *similia similibus curantur* and very much keeps within the spirit of the 'As above, so below,' maxim.

You need to practice this before actually using it on a real spell because everyone reacts differently to the weather. For example, some people see snow and immediately want to go out and build a snowman or play snowballs. Others head straight for the fireside. So your personal reaction to different types of weather will influence your breathing which in turn will affect the way you send your intention out into the world. As you experiment remember to keep records in your notebook so you can always refer to them. The idea is to find a pattern that makes you feel completely attuned to whatever weather pattern you're using.

Begin by noticing the weather. Any weather. Rain, sun, wind - they all affect how we breathe. Usually it's so subtle we don't notice and our bodies make the adjustments automatically for us. In very cold weather, the freezing air hurts our lungs so we automatically breathe in through the nose and our breathing becomes shallower. On a bright warm day, however, we can breathe deeply and easily although once the temperature starts to rise our breathing becomes shallow and quick. Make notes of all these things, how you breathe, what feels most comfortable (and conversely, what feels downright unpleasant) according to the weather on any given day. You should soon notice a pattern.

Begin with relatively stable weather for your first exercises. If possible, sit outside or at least near a window where you can observe the weather for yourself. I find that cloudy, overcast days with little breeze have equal inhaled and exhaled breaths whereas windy days require an exhaled breath that is twice as long as the inhaled breath. Bright, calm summer days require long, soft exhaled breaths like gentle sighs.

Remember always that you're working *with* the weather, don't try to control it.

Now project your breath towards the weather. Feel yourself breathing into it, as though you've become part of the elements around you. Just as the weather influences your breathing, so it's important to feel at one with it. By understanding these subtle changes we can turn them to our advantage. Some people feel uneasy with this, feeling that we are somehow 'taking advantage' of the elements. It's not like that at all. Weather is far too powerful for us to take advantage of it, and magic is neither good nor bad, it just *is*. It's the intention behind the spell that creates good or bad results.

Using the weather in your magic has a number of advantages. Firstly weather is ever-present; we never have a day without it. Secondly weather is always changing and is therefore new each time you use it. Thirdly, if you do have several days of very similar weather remember that the weather will always work with you *once you have found an interpretation that fits your purpose*. Try thinking of it as *novena* magic (from the Latin *novem* meaning number nine). In the Roman Catholic Church a novena consists of prayers over a nine day period in order to obtain certain requests, which derives from the earlier, pagan Roman tradition of nine days for religious celebrations or the nine days of mourning observed by the ancient Greeks. If you have several days of similar weather, then build up your spell gradually, day by day to increase its power.

To find the best way to interpret every sort of weather in order to use it in your magic, you must first decide what the different types of weather mean *to you*. For example, some people regard storms as threatening, fearing damage to trees and property, whereas another person might remember falling passionately in love during a storm and forever associate storms with desire. Generally speaking a storm is good for any spell requiring strong energy such as healing, travel, work, study and love spells, or some invocations.

High winds are good for spells that need to travel a long distance. Spells for people in distant countries or cities, or spells bearing messages are all suitable for windy days because they will literally blow your spell to the recipient. Wind is also good for banishing. For this you'll need to envisage the wind blowing something away from whomever or whatever you are trying to protect. Wind is also ideal for any spell that aims to bring about the end of something. The old saying to 'blow the cobwebs away' is particularly apt when describing wind. When you want to get rid of bad habits or emotional baggage, use the wind to carry them as far away as possible.

Weather can be endlessly adapted for your spells. You can use any type of weather provided you can find a way of working with it. For example, imagine you have a much-loved relative who has gone to live in a town some miles away. You have spoken to them on the phone and they are lonely and tearful. Outside the weather is wet and windy. You can work with this, visualising the wind carrying your love and support to your relative and blowing their sorrow away, while the rain is beating down the barriers that are preventing them from settling. Rain doesn't always have to mean tears! Simply adjust your breathing according to the weather, until you feel that you, the rain and the wind are all in harmony and working as one. Sometimes, especially in the early days, it helps to say what the weather is actually doing:

The wind blows, the rain beats down

When you say this, you must listen to the wind and imagine it blowing the problems away and carrying your love and support to the person you want to help. Also, as you say 'the wind blows' breathe out very firmly, as though you are about to whistle, imagining that you are breathing right into the middle of the wind. Your breath and the wind will merge, become one and blow right across the landscape. It can also help to work out your compass bearings. If your relative lives north of you, stand facing that direction so that you're literally breathing towards her. Anything you can do to help push your magic along then give it a try.

Wind can also be used to encourage communication between two people. For this you need a long, steady out breath to propel the spell forwards, while imagining the wind literally *pushing* the desired communication ahead. An uneven, ragged breath will only result in the spell blowing this way and that and ending up anywhere other than its required destination.

Whenever you use the wind, you can also add in a written spell or verse. This isn't essential – your breath, intention and willpower will do all that is needed – but sometimes people like to have something spell-like to say. So as you imagine propelling the spell forwards, you can say something like:

> By the wind's power
> Send this spell
> Straight as an arrow
> Guard it well

Alternatively just direct your thoughts as 'I use the power of the wind to send this spell to [say what you want it to do, or whom you want it to protect]'

As you begin to speak (or mentally direct your spell), your hands should be together in front of you, palms together, fingers pointing upwards. Then slowly extend your arms, gradually separating your hands until they are no more than a foot apart. This is in order to keep the breath together, so that it doesn't get blown to pieces the moment it and the wind come into contact with each other. The very best magic makes use of imagining the reasons behind the words and actions. Indeed, gestures have been part of traditional magic since Ancient Egypt and often can be far more effective than words.

When you have finished speaking, breathe out slowly, with your tongue pressing hard against the lower teeth. You are aiming for an 'almost there' wind in the tunnel sound, not quite a proper whistle. (Whistling has traditionally been associated with raising storms and high winds) This spell requires one of the strongest out breaths you will need to do, and is ideal even for those who have never got the knack of whistling!

As in everything you do using Magic on the Breath, keep any words and thoughts as simple and clear as possible. All you need is a strong will and steady, controlled breathing. If you really feel the need of a rhyming spell, try something like:

> *By the power of wind and sea*
> *I [name] send healing thoughts to thee [name]*

You could also try:

> *West wind full of rain*
> *Heal (Name) remove his/her pain*
> *As you wash the mud and dirt*
> *Cleanse his/her illness, heal his/her hurt.*

A stiff breeze (as opposed to a howling gale which is unpredictable) is good for spells when a relationship is over and you want to move on as quickly and cleanly as possible. Traditionally the element of air is associated with intelligence and intellect, especially in problem solving. In classical mythology, air was associated with the Roman god Mercury and the Greek Hermes, both messengers of the gods. In a spent relationship where passion has gone, the cool logic of air will be an ideal helper. Pay particular attention to precise breathing in this type of spell so that the relationship ends with minimal fuss and bother.

Some people notice a connection between their own mood and the weather, for example that it rains whenever they feel sad. Certainly a sudden downpour is likely to feel like a flood of tears if you're already feeling unhappy. Wet weather can be good for spells to banish melancholy. You begin with the heavens crying in harmony with you and banish the sorrow as the weather improves. Showers are gentler and can be used for general purification rituals. Water is closely associated the moon, so if you happen to have a rainy day coincide with a full moon you will be using the elements at their most potent.

Cloudy days are good for spells that deal in secrets. As the clouds clear, so secrets are revealed, and also vice versa, as the skies become cloudy, something may be hidden. There are different types of cloud, just as there are different types of secrets. The great grey or white *cumulus* clouds that billow across the sky are quite different from the shapeless thick curtains of *stratus* cloud that turn the sky a shade of dull grey. *Cumulus* clouds are ever changing, full of surprises; *stratus* are sluggish and all enveloping, they are particularly good for keeping things hidden. Fog and mist can be used in spells to reveal or hide the truth.

Sometimes people ask me, 'What should I say?' and my answer is always, 'Say what is in your heart, say what you mean, say what you want or need.' There are no 'right' words, only truth. If you really feel at a lost, jot down a basic two line rhyming invocation to get you started, something like:

> Clouds that hide the sun from view,
> Reveal to me what I must do

Then forget making any more rhymes and just state your purpose. In my experience, magic has a built in insincerity detector!

Sunny weather is good for love spells, especially if you regard the object of your affections as the light of your life! The breathing best suited for love spells is usually a half sigh, in and out through the mouth. You will have to experiment to see what sort of rhythm suits you best, but usually the breath in equals the breath out. On the last word of the final line you need to exhale to a soft 'aaah' sound. The wind should then take the spell and deliver it to its target.

However, sunny days aren't essential for love magic. Rain is closely associated with strong emotions, so there's no reason you shouldn't perform a love spell in wet weather. Magic is all about using what is to hand creatively! The sun is also closely associated with the element of fire, and with the emotions of love and anger. It is also closely linked to St Michael, Lord of the Sun who appears in the Biblical Book of Revelations fighting dragons. Working on this imagery a sunny day could be a great choice for spells that require you to overcome difficult odds. In this case you may need to imagine the heat of the sun as the dragon's breath on you.

Sunshine is also good for healing spells. The sun was traditionally regarded as a great healer back in ancient times and the ancient Greeks and Romans regarded the god Apollo as a sun god and god of healing (amongst other things). When I was young I was told to 'go and sit in the sun' if I had been feeling run down or unwell. Nowadays I often use my memories of its warmth and wellbeing for my own healing spells.

At this stage start thinking about how you define yourself. We use words like 'I', 'me' or 'my' quite often in magic, but what exactly do we mean? Sometimes it pays to stop and think about who you are and how you view yourself. Our names don't really define us, since hardly anyone has a name so unusual that nobody else shares it. So what is it that makes us the person we are? For this exercise, take a sheet of paper and write down how you view yourself. Never mind what others might think, this is your personal viewpoint. List your strengths and weaknesses, how you fit into your family or community. Don't try and write an essay, just jot down the words that come to mind.

Then take another sheet and draw a stick figure in the centre of the page. This represents you, so write your initials just underneath the figure. Now draw other figures (with their initials) around your figure, thinking about how you all link together. For example, if you feel you are at the centre of your family you should draw stick figures representing these people all around your central figure.

On the other hand, if you feel like an outsider you should draw the rest of your family down in the corner. Even though your stick figure is still in the centre of the page, you will see that you are on the periphery of the family. Next take a new page for all the relationships that are important to you, family, work, friends, etc. Are you always on the periphery or sometimes central?

Love spells in particular require not only that you be free from negativity but also that you have a good sense of your own identity. Many a spell has been ruined because its creator was so vague, or so negative, the only magic she achieved was to send the object of her affections into the arms of someone else! To give you an example, I once held a workshop where someone wanted to catch the attention of someone she admired for some time from afar. She stuck to my advice about keeping everything simple and wrote:

Tell him I love him…

This was a lovely thought but I explained the importance of identifying the 'I' and 'him' in the spell otherwise the object of our affection may think that someone else loves him. After some thought she came back with her next attempt:

Tell John I really do love him,

which still didn't quite address the problem! Of course, if you are simply reaffirming love that *already* exists between two people, for example, husband and wife, you don't need to worry so much about identifying yourself. However, if you are trying to fan the flames of a new love then you should at least say your own name at some point during the spell. Eventually the student came up with:

Tell John that I, Lucy, love him.
Tell him I desire him to love me as I love him,
Tell him my heart beats as one with his own,
Winds of the compass points,
Tell John to say that he loves me.

She was worried that there were no rhymes in her spell, but the result was so heartfelt that it wasn't necessary. There is a great deal of argument about the ethics of casting loves spells and it's true they're not always wise or appropriate. However, love spells have been around since the beginning of human civilisation. Since we're never going to prevent people from casting them, the least we can do is to make sure they cast them properly so there's less chance of mistakes. Not everyone is a gormless fool who casts love spells at people they worship from afar. Sometimes – admittedly they are rare – there are good reasons for casting a love spell.

And love itself is a funny old thing. Sometimes it moves into our lives whether we invite it in or not. When I was about fourteen, I woke up one summer's night feeling that someone was calling me. I was convinced this was my soul mate, even though I had no idea of his identity. My teenage years passed, and I never met him. I even began to believe I must have been mistaken although the experience was remains vivid to this day. Maybe I should have had more faith, but time went by and my cynicism became obstinate. I even married and had a child.

Then one day I met *him,* and I knew. It was the same voice I'd heard that night. And it was strange but on the day we met he also had a strange experience, hearing a voice telling him that 'Today will change your life.'

Sometimes love itself seems to cast the spell.

Chapter Nine
Knot Magic

Sometimes we come across magical traditions so ancient and so widespread that we realise they must have originated with our very earliest ancestors. Knots for example, are so prehistoric we have no idea who first used them, or who invented them. They predate the plough and the wheel by tens of thousands of years occurring in all cultures, right across the world. And in every continent they are associated with magic.

Knot spells are an excellent type of magic for beginners. They require no special skills other than tying a simple knot in a piece of string, which is also a handy aid concentration - think of tying a knot in a handkerchief in order to remember something! When done well, knot spells can be so effective you may never want to try anything else.

It's easy to underestimate the value of knots nowadays because we don't use them much in our daily life. We fasten our clothes with zips and buttons, and use rivets, nails, screws and glue to join things together. Most of us only use knots for nowadays in shoelaces, tying fancy bows on presents and tying up our rubbish sacks (always supposing our local council hasn't provided a wheelie bin.)

Our ancestors however used knots in every way imaginable, tying on their fishing hooks, axe heads and even the fletching (feathers) on medieval arrowheads. Wooden scaffolding was lashed together with ropes, ships depended on their rigging. Any knot that didn't fulfil its purpose could quite literally kill. Little wonder then that they were invested with magical power. After all, to take two pieces of rope and knot them together so that they become in effect a single unit is a form of transformation in itself.

Understanding how knots were used in the past helps us work out how to adapt them for our own use. A great deal of knowledge and experience were laid down in ancient times but subsequently lost or misinterpreted. Indeed in some countries, even the words for magic were closely linked to knots: in Russia, one of the words for a wizard is *Uzol'nik* meaning 'one who ties knots' while in Hebrew literature, someone who practices magic is called *hober haber* meaning 'someone who ties magical knots.' The Finns were said to be particularly good at harnessing the winds. One of their ancient legends told of a smith who kept a knotted rope in his forge, each knot containing a storm.

One of the most popular magical uses for knots was to control the weather, especially the wind. Homer, the ancient Greek poet, tells how Aeolus, King of the Winds, gave Odysseus a leather bag containing all the winds except the west wind to help him sail home. The crew, however, were convinced the bag contained treasure and opened it when Odysseus was asleep. The winds escaped all at once raising a great storm and instead of taking the ship home sent it straight back to Aeolus' island.

Years ago sailors would buy magic strings bearing three knots. If their ship was becalmed (a serious problem back in the days before steam powered vessels) they could undo the first knot and conjure up a gentle wind. If that wasn't enough, the second knot would bring a stronger wind, and the third brought forth a veritable storm.

Other methods of obtaining a favourable wind included wrapping the wind in the corner of a napkin or sack which was released when opened. Even boiling a kettle could raise a storm. Seaports often had thriving communities of 'wind brokers' who offered to control the strength of the wind if not its direction. Some were accused of giving favourable winds to their friends and howling gales to their enemies! In fourth century Constantinople, a man called Sopater was executed for becalming ships that should have carried grain to the city's starving inhabitants.

Being able to control the weather could also be regarded as something of a threat, however. Indeed it's possible that witches were blamed for a series of poor harvests in the late Middle Ages, which ultimately brought about the witch persecutions in Europe. This isn't as far-fetched as it seems; we have put men on the moon but cannot stop a tsunami or a hurricane. Like our medieval ancestors, we are still at the weather's mercy. It's surprising there isn't more interest in weather magic in the western world. Very few people seem to practise it any more, although one of my aunts did weather spells as recently as the late 1950's.

Knot magic however does have other uses apart from controlling the weather. It can be used for healing, protection, fertility and even summoning spirits. It can even operate after a specified lapse of time, and at a great distance. Understandably, centuries ago people began to fear knots and a great deal of folklore grew up around them, especially at weddings.

From a practical point of view, natural fibres make the best knots. Jute is ideal, but cotton or woollen threads of the type used for knitting and crochet work will also do. In ancient times knots could be tied in twigs, straws or even hair, and sometimes the cord was knotted around the branch or trunk of a tree. My own preference is for natural colours if possible, because I feel these absorb your energies more than those that have been dyed, especially if synthetic dyes were used. Self dyed cords, especially using dyes made from plants with magical properties conducive to the spell, would be especially powerful however.

Nowadays most people use string or fine rope, but you can always experiment with other materials if you prefer and also with a variety of colours. Seven thousand years ago in Babylonia magicians tied knots in twisted cords comprising one white and one black thread. This colour scheme was also used in Scotland in healing spells when the cord was knotted and bound around a damaged limb. Red cords were used for healing spells and magic intended to protect against the Evil Eye.

Most people use a single cord, although some prefer to twist or plait several together. The British Museum possesses a formula for a Babylonian healing knot spell that requires three threads plaited together with fourteen knots (twice seven.) Most spells requires either three, seven or nine knots, since these were sacred numbers in most ancient societies. In Romania nine knots were used in a healing spell to cure a bad back. Each knot specified an area of the body to be freed from pain and when the spell was complete the cord had thrown into running water to carry it far away from the patient. If it was thrown into a well however, anyone drinking from it would suffer the original illness! Other numbers are possible however if you prefer.

What the Romanian example shows us is that the magic is caught up in the knot. Sometimes the cord has to be preserved but at other times it must be destroyed presumably to set the intention free. It really all depends on the type of spell. For example, one old method wart charming involves tying a knot for each wart you wish to remove. Some people like to rub each knot on the wart it represents in order to set up a physical link. Magically the essence of the wart is transferred to the cord and the knots represent cutting off the blood supply to the wart which will kill it. Traditionally in this charm the cord has to be burned immediately afterwards –by destroying the cord you magically destroy the warts.

For other cures however, it was important that the cord remained intact. Some magicians advised wearing the knotted cord (usually around the neck) for as long as possible, suggesting that it not only had the power to cure but also to protect. If you really can't face wearing a piece of string round your neck you must find some other way of disposing of it, don't just leave it lying around to attract negative energies. For as long as the knot remains tied, the magic is active.

The close association between knots and breathing are longstanding. For example, if dealing with contagious illnesses the spell caster (*not* the patient!) would breathe upon the knots. This magically 'fixed' the spell in the knot. In Egypt there is a tradition of blowing upon a cord containing seven knots in order to cure a cold - a classic example of using the breath to harness one's magical will.

For thousands of years, people have believed that knots can influence the fertility of crops, animals and people. In ancient Greece and Rome brides knotted their girdles to ensure they would have children, and the husband had to undo the knot before the marriage was consummated. This may well be the origin of the old saying 'to tie the knot' meaning to get married. Knot spells have an endless range of uses, and you shouldn't be fooled by their apparent simplicity – they are very powerful indeed.

For example, many years ago, I wrote a spell for a friend who had complained that she needed more confidence. Her children had left home and she felt people had been taking her for granted. I was probably a bit naïve and should have told her to get out of the house more and find some hobbies, but I took what she said at face value and wrote a spell designed to give her some confidence – what I would call a 'self affirmation spell.' I chose a knot spell because it was easy to perform, even for a complete beginner.

I never, in my wildest dreams, anticipated what would happen next. She threw her husband out of the house, took up with a string (no pun intended!) of boyfriends and got herself a new job. You see, when she asked me for a spell, she knew *precisely* what she wanted, and although the spell I wrote was for self affirmation, when she performed it for herself she envisaged the changes she wanted to make. This is always this danger when writing spells for other people: they are not always totally honest about their real intentions. Sometimes they're not even honest with themselves. It's like the old saying, 'Be very careful what you pray for – you might get it.'

From my friend's point of view, the spell did exactly what she wanted at the time although I can't honestly say that it made her any happier in the long term, and I suspect it caused quite a bit of heartbreak all around. But these results were due to what went on in her head when she was performing the spell rather than what I wrote. She didn't tell me until much later that she'd wanted to leave her husband for years.

That experience taught me a very important lesson: if we write a spell based on false or incomplete information it will almost certainly produce unexpected - and sometimes unwanted - results. Whatever magical technique you choose for your magic, always be honest with yourself - and others. If you're not then the laws of unintended consequences have a way of teaching us some memorable lessons!

You should also avoid writing a spell and then rushing off to perform it unless you are faced with a real emergency. If you are trying to solve a problem, chances are it will still be there after you've given it some thought. If possible – especially if you're writing your own spell – put it aside for a day or so and then return to it. This isn't just to allow you to 'cool off.' Often you'll find that writing the spell will allow your subconscious mind to start dealing with the situation.

Taking time to step back also gives you the opportunity to spot and deal with any ambiguous wording. Having reviewed the spell and decided you want to go ahead, choose a time when you'll have enough peace and quiet. Ideally you will need no more than ten to fifteen minutes for most spells using Magic on the Breath. It's not a great deal of time, but it has to be yours and yours alone. I've often got up at a ridiculously early hour to perform a spell simply because I know it's the one time of day when I can be completely uninterrupted.

If you've never tried a knot spell before, try starting with a self affirmation spell. This is magic designed to bring out the best in you, to develop your character. Begin by making a list of the things you would like to achieve personally, habits you would like to break, ambitions you want to fulfil. Which ones are really important to you? Pick nine that you feel are most important. Don't worry if you can't think of nine things – use seven or three if you prefer. Don't be tempted to include any old thing just to make up the numbers. If you do plan to have nine affirmations however, the third, seventh and ninth ones will be slightly longer than the others to reflect the special magical qualities of these numbers.

To carry out the spell you'll need a length of string or cord. The length is entirely a matter of personal choice but remember that the thicker the string, the longer it will have to be in order to give you room to tie the required number of knots. Personally I like to use garden twine and experiment with various lengths until I find something that suits my purpose (and my knotting skills). Don't be afraid to practice, especially in placing the knots along the string. There's nothing more annoying than getting to the final affirmation and finding you've run out of space! If you can, keep the string close to you so that it absorbs some of your personal energies. Tuck it in your pocket or your rucksack. Put it under your pillow or leave it on your windowsill on a moonlit night. Breathe on it from time to time too, the sort of warm exhaled breath you use when you're trying to mist up a mirror. This will transfer the essence of your Self into the string to empower it. The extra time spent empowering your string has another purpose too, it gives you time to mull over the affirmations and make sure you're happy with them.

Get everything you will need for the spell together in one place. This may sound as though I'm stating the blatantly obvious, but you'd be surprised how many people break off in the middle of a spell to go and hunt for scissors, candles, matches or whatever. Don't forget your list of affirmations – always write them down otherwise there's a good chance you'll end up casting a spell for something quite different from your original intention!

You will also need to have some idea what you are going to do with the cord once you're finished. Basically your main choices are to wear it, burn it, bury it or throw it into running water. Another way of looking at it is to decide which element is most appropriate, fire and air (burning), earth (burying) or water? Whichever method you decide to use, you should dispose of the cord quickly afterwards. Don't leave it hanging around for a couple of hours while you drive to the nearest river, dig a hole or build a bonfire. Get everything ready first, and then do the spell. Good preparation is the key to successful magic.

When you're ready, clear some space for yourself. You do this not because you need a lot of room to perform the spell – quite the opposite in fact, you could probably perform it in a matchbox! – but because you need to be in an area clear of negative energies. This doesn't mean spring cleaning your home from top to bottom. A cleared and dusted space on a worktop will do. People often imagine their magic will suffer if they don't have a special '*Majick Room*' complete with purpose built altar and velvet robes! It won't. Most of us have always struggled to cast spells in the midst of family life, with newspapers, toys, pets, people and the TV all competing for any available space. That's just life and we have to deal with it.

In the midst of clearing a space, collecting string and writing affirmations it's all too easy to forget that we need to prepare ourselves too. This doesn't mean you have to rush off and soak in a bath of essential oils surrounded by a dozen candles. You can if you wish, but you don't have to. What I'm talking about here is taking time to ground yourself and set up a steady breathing rhythm. To really think about your intention. Although high emotion and energy can be invaluable for propelling some spells, a knot spell is best worked with steady, calm determination.

Important: *The only time your magic really suffers is when you don't make a proper space for it in your heart and mind. You have to give it your full attention because it deserves nothing less. If you try to cast a spell while wondering whether you forgot to turn the kettle off, all that distraction will rub off on your magic. Just as you should keep your mind on the road when you're driving, so you should keep your mind on your intention when casting spells.*

Some people like to work consistently from one end of the string to the other. Personally I prefer to begin by tying the first knot in the centre of the string, the second at the left end, the third at the right, and then tie the others in the remaining spaces. You need to space them roughly equidistant, but don't agonise over this. As you tie each knot, you will need to recite the appropriate part of the spell, for the first knot you say the first affirmation, for the second knot the second affirmation and so on. After each affirmation, breathe on the knot you have just tied. This is a suggested set of affirmations, just to give you an idea and act as a template:

1. By the power of this knot, I shall learn to know myself.
2. By the power of this knot, I will be the person I am meant to be.
3. By the power of this knot, I shall be appreciated by others for what I am, not for what I could or should or ought to be but *what I am*.
4. By the power of this knot, I will be truly loved, for myself.
5. By the power of this knot, I will be tolerant of others.
6. By the power of this knot, I will learn to live for every hour of every day.

7. By the power of this knot, I will confront my darkest fears, drag them out into the light and vanquish them utterly.

8. By the power of this knot, I will be protected against those who wish me harm.

9. By the power of this knot, I will have my hopes and dreams and others shall not take them from me or trample them underfoot. *I will have my hopes and dreams.*

Normally I don't recommend phrases such as 'I will be' in a spell because they don't specify a given time frame. However, in this type of affirmation spell tying the knots is itself an act that grounds you firmly in the present anyway. Once you have finished reciting the spell, spit on the cord – it may sound disgusting but spitting has been an integral part of knot magic all over the world for thousands of years. In Lapland, witches used to tie three knots in a towel then spit on them while Arabs believed that witches spat and blew on knots. Magically speaking, spitting helps to convey a vital part of your essence of self to the knot.

Next gather up the cord in your hands and breathe on it, saying 'This is my will, *fiat.*' [*Fiat* is Latin and roughly translates as 'so be it' or 'let it be so'.] This is my own preference but you could use something else such as 'So mote it be' or 'This is my will, this is my wish,' or whatever you feel most comfortable with. If you do decide to use *fiat*, remember that it's pronounced fi-at (the first syllable rhyming with eye not ee). It's not supposed to sound like the car manufacturer!

You don't have to say anything while disposing of the cord. Just get on with it. There are many times in magic when complete silence is necessary and this is one of them! Afterwards, take a few minutes to unwind, breathing deeply and grounding yourself. Then go off and do something mundane like having a cup of tea and forget about it. Once a spell is over it's done. Set it free. Otherwise you'll stop it from working properly.

Knot spells can be used in much the same way for healing. Again I would recommend using nine knots and repeating 'I will be well' because this helps drive the spell by reminding you of your main intention. As with everything in this book, you should adapt it for your own needs.

1. By the power of this knot, I will be well.
2. By the power of this knot, I will walk and move without pain.
3. By the power of this knot, I will be well.
4. By the power of this knot, I will sleep soundly and peacefully at night.
5. By the power of this knot, I will laugh and smile.
6. By the power of this knot, I will learn to do those things that will make me well.
7. By the power of this knot, I will be well
8. By the power of this knot, I shall look forward to a bright and better future.
9. By the power of this knot, I banish pain and sickness, and I will be well and enjoy my life.

Again you will see I have used 'I will' in this spell. If you want to specify a given time that's fine, but healing often takes longer than we would like. You can always change this to 'I will soon be well again' if you prefer. You can even specify a given time frame, 'I will be well by this time next year.' It's really a matter of personal choice although it's important to remember that magic cannot solve all our problems. We have to do everything physically possible to give the spell a helping hand too.

Important: *People sometimes claim that if you are ill or on any kind of medication that you should not perform magic. This is absolute nonsense. The only proviso I would make is that if you personally feel too tired to perform a spell you should put it off until you feel brighter. If your will and your intention are sound, then your magic will be likewise.*

It's also important as you become more skilled at casting spells that you learn to resist requests to cast them for other people. Partly this is because it is much better to teach them to cast their own spells; magic done on our own behalf is always much more effective than when someone else casts a spell for us. Good spells take time, effort and energy to create. If you become bogged down in doing spells for others, especially those who are too lazy to help themselves, you'll end up a wreck within a couple of months. Worse, when you look back, you'll realise that many of the spells that drained you weren't even necessary!

Finally, it's worth taking a brief look at binding spells. These are often confused with knot spells, although they are quite different. Binding spells are intended to bring things or people together *and keep them there*. Even though you can untie or cut these spells, their original purpose was usually permanent and many people dislike binding spells for precisely this reason. It's hard to know whether what we want so badly this week will seem as important to us next week or next year let alone in twelve years' time. They are commonly regarded as negative, perhaps because they were so often used in love spells to bind two people together, or in hexes where they hinder someone's free will in order to harm them. However binding spells can also be used positively, for example in business ventures or uniting people with the subjects they are studying.

Like all magic, binding spells should never be undertaken without sensible consideration of the implications. This is why I try to teach the principles and mechanics of spell crafting rather than just giving you a book of spells. Magic will not work properly without effort and intelligence. Learning how to cast spells takes time, energy, willpower and hard work. There is no quick fix. You either accept that, or you leave spell casting well alone.

It's as simple as that.

Chapter Ten
Magic and the Moon.

Years ago when my children were very young, we were walking home together beneath a radiant full moon. Well, *I* was walking – the others were taking it in turns to argue about whose turn it was to ride in the one and only pushchair. My middle daughter, who was about two, suddenly looked up and pointed at the sky.

'Look. Moon.'

We all stopped struggling over the pushchair for a moment and looked up. Above us the stars twinkled in a velvet dark sky and plump full moon smiled down at us.

'It's *my* moon,' said the eldest, promptly, 'I saw it first.'

The moon has that effect on us. We all belong to it and in some strange way it belongs to each of us too.

And this is strange because it is the sun that's so vital to our existence, while the moon seems to be just a chunk of dead rock trapped in the earth's orbit. But the moon is benign; we even can look at it without endangering our eyesight. It exerts its power over our planet, the seas, plants, even people and animals. It's probably no co-incidence that the word lunatic comes from the Latin word *luna* meaning moon. Traditionally it's the full moon that gets people agitated or behaving out of character, but the new moon can also have marked effects on us.

I remember one of my uncles trying to teach me how to navigate by the stars. I was only about eight years old so it was a pretty tall order, and no matter how he tried, I just couldn't recognise the Plough, Orion the Hunter or any of the famous constellations. But the moon is different – you can't miss it. And you can't miss how it changes shape either. Look at it over the course of a month (twenty eight and a quarter days to be precise), and you'll see that it changes from crescent to full and back again. There are even days when it disappears altogether. These are called moon phases. The sun, by comparison is always a fierce, glowing disc in the sky. It may change colour, especially at sunset, but it never changes its shape.

In magic people often pay great attention to moon phases, believing that the 'correct' moon phase is essential for the success of the spell. In practice it really depends on the type of magic you're trying to perform. In elaborate ceremonial or ritual magic, you must work with Tables of Correspondences that set out the correct planet, colour, plant, incense, metal, symbolic creature, and planetary spirit for every hour of the day and night, and every day of the week and month. Obviously if you're trying to get all these things to correspond, you'll need to take moon phases into account since this sort of magic relies on quite subtle but complex vibrations; it doesn't take much to twist them out of shape.

However, the drawback of *starting off* with this type of magic is that it can cause a sort of magical paralysis. You exert so much effort and energy on getting the correspondences just right that you never get chance to do any real magic. It doesn't seep into your bones in the way that the best magic should. The same thing can happen if you slavishly work with moon phases.

With Magic on the Breath, you are trying to free yourself from unnecessary restrictions. Yes, it would be wonderful if we could always have just the right moon phase etc., for casting our spell, but life isn't like that. And we have to be careful not to hem ourselves around with so many restrictions that we never actually get around to doing anything. Too much observance of moon phases and astrological hours can become a really good excuse not to do any magic at all.

It might seem strange to be so fearful but you'd be surprised how many people feel this way. They end up worrying unnecessarily: Is it the right time? Should I wait for a more appropriate hour? In the end nothing gets done. Newcomers are particularly prone to this. While some are wildly over enthusiastic and will start casting spells to try and stop the milk curdling, others will look for any and every excuse never to cast a spell at all.

So let's look at the main ideas about moon phases and get them into some sort of perspective. Moon phases are important to some types of magic but not all, and if it's the only thing preventing you casting your spell you should look for ways around it. Believe me, there is almost always a way of resolving any magical problem. You will probably be told at some time or another that spells intended to cause an increase should *only* be done when the moon is waxing while spells to cause decrease should only be attempted when it's waning. Actually none of this is written in stone. Moon phases should never prevent us doing magic, but they may influence *how* we do it. We just have to learn to manipulate the intention.

For a healing spell, for example, you might choose a waxing moon to ensure an increase in health. But suppose the moon is waning and you simply don't have time to wait? *In that case look for what you can decrease instead.* For example, you could cast your healing spell with the intention of making temperature or pain decrease. This way you can at least try *something* without having to wait a few weeks for the correct moon phase.

Here are some other examples of how to manipulate you intention to suit the moon phase:
- On a waxing moon you can do a spell to increase your love of studying. On a waning moon adjust the intention to decrease the number of times you forget to do your homework or allow your mind to wander.
- On a waxing moon you can do a spell to increase wealth (yours or someone else's). On a waning moon do a spell to decrease poverty.
- On a waxing moon do a spell to gain a promotion. On a waning moon do a spell to prevent being taken for granted in your present position.
- On a waxing moon do a spell to gain a better new job. On a waning moon do a spell to decrease the competition you will face applying for the job.
- On a waning moon do a spell to banish negativity. On a waxing moon adapt this to attract more positivity into your life.

Admittedly, the spells are not identical, although the overall intention is very similar. You should certainly try it whenever you don't have the luxury of waiting a week or so for the 'right' moon phase.

Some of the examples I've given above are clearly spells that will benefit us, and there are those who will throw their hands up in horror at this point, crying, 'You should never do magic for personal gain!' Actually this is a relatively new idea, and yet another attempt to hem us in with rules and regulations that have little bearing on reality or even tradition. Most people's everyday lives are spent pursuing personal gain and it doesn't do them, or those around them any harm. *It only becomes a problem when they cease to pursue anything else.* Or when it warps how they interact with the rest of the world.

Most of the time there's absolutely nothing wrong with wanting a new job. Nor is there anything wrong with doing a spell to reduce the competition and (presumably) increase your chances. The other candidates may change their minds, decide it's not suitable for them after all or be offered an even *better* job. So there's nothing wrong, on the face of it, with trying to persuade the competition that they don't want the job. What you don't do however is cast spells to cause the competition harm – any more than you would physically try and trip them up if you met them at the interview.

The main reason you try and avoid actively causing harm when possible – apart from the fact that it's highly anti-social and sometimes illegal - is that if you start on this kind of magic you will never be able to leave it alone. I call it hexing, some call it the dark or left hand path. It is highly addictive. Also since most types of magic – for good *and* bad - rebound to a greater or lesser extent upon their makers, the more harmful your intention, the more unpleasant the psychic fall-out.

My family performed hexes virtually all the time. Anything that got in their way, anyone they didn't like (often for quite trivial reasons) and they hexed them. It wasn't good for their victims, but it wasn't good for them either. Believe me, that sort of magic *does* attract its own kind of punishment though sometimes not as quickly as it deserves.

If you decide to work with a moon phase, you have to start off by checking how the moon looks on the day you intend to cast the spell. When I was young that meant going outside when it was dark and looking up at the skies. It could be very frustrating on wet and windy nights when it was simply too cloudy to see anything. Nowadays you can check online on one of the many moon phase calendars without needing to even set foot outside the door. This can be helpful because there is only a single day which is the true full moon, even though it can look full to the naked eye for several days. Even more confusingly, the moon disappears for several days, just before the new crescent moon becomes visible, so don't be surprised if you go out of doors on a clear night and can't see it!

The moon has long been regarded as female, in spite of the 'Man in the Moon' nursery rhymes. Each cycle of the moon, from the new to the dark, therefore has a subtle yet powerful feminine element. Traditionally the 'dark of the moon' belonged to the ancient Greek goddess Hekate, and this moon phase is good for spells that emphasise endings, or the passage from life to death.

Whatever name you choose to call her, the Moon Goddess is a wise teacher, mistress of renewal and mystery, guardian of secrets. Even when you cannot see the moon, she is there. Address her with respect, remembering that though you cannot see her, she can certainly see you. Magic on the Breath is ideal for this type of work, because all you really need is a true heart, not elaborate ritual. Experience has taught me that the moon is at her most powerful during lunar eclipses.

None of us can just demand what we want and expect to get it just like that. You have to be patient which is probably the real significance of using moon phases. For that reason moon magic does not lend itself to 'quick fix' spells but is better for spells intended to take effect over a longer period of time. Also you need a certain mental agility in order to manipulate your intention to fit the moon phase. Luckily, getting to know the moon is quite easy provided you accept that it's a lifetime's work. I often think of it as paying court to the moon, bowing to her in all her phases, getting to know her various guises (a moon seen near the horizon appears absolutely enormous!)

The new moon is ideal for spells dealing with new beginnings, for example, to ensure or protect a new love, moving into a new house, a new phase in your life, new job, a new era of better health etc. The ancient Greeks believed the new moon was a good time for marriages and that children born then would be lucky. The Druids believed that the moon symbolised prosperity, with fortune increasing or decreasing according to whether it was waxing, full or waning. Because of the way it changes shape, the moon has long been associated with increase and decrease, growth and decay. Some people even claimed that washing clothes on a waning moon removed the dirt more effectively!

Important: *You may not be able to change the moon phase, but you can almost always manipulate your intention to suit whatever the moon phase happens to be.*

Another technique is to just forget about moon's phase and instead use the moon as a focus, gazing up at it using controlled breathing and a simple, straightforward request. It doesn't have to be a full moon although many people feel more comfortable when the moon is a shape they actually recognise, such as round or crescent shaped rather than gibbous (which is some way between the two and looks like a lop-sided football.)

The full moon is very powerful, and beginners in particular need to be aware that its energies can take the unwary on a real roller coaster ride. When you cast your spell, get out and look at the moon, grounding yourself and using soft controlled breathing throughout. You should aim to inhale and exhale through the mouth on a very soft 'haaah' sound before presenting your request. I always like to finish with words to the effect of 'I leave it with you.'

If we're going to do magic that relies upon or invokes the moon's power, then it goes without saying that we need to get to know her. I have known people spend ages poring over almanacs and various charts that set out precise moon phases and planetary positions yet who rarely spend any time outside in the moon's company. You can't treat it like some vague concept and expect to work with it successfully.

The moon is as real as you or I, the cat on the wall or the shop at the end of the street. When you go out into the dark and gaze at it, you are echoing the practices of hundreds, thousands and tens of thousands of years. These vibrations of wonder have been generated over a span of time almost as ancient as Mankind itself. Even knowing that man has walked on the moon doesn't detract from this. If anything, it can make us feel that the power of the moon, built up over millennia, is even more accessible if only we reach out and try to touch it. But I can only give suggestions that have worked for me. By all means try them, but if they don't work for you don't be afraid to experiment with others.

A good way to start is to salute the moon. I don't mean a military style salute although if it feels appropriate to you, by all means give it a try. 'Saluting the moon' can be interpreted in many ways. You can bow, curtsey or even just wave if you prefer. Some people like to bow to a new moon, usually nine times. Others perform the same action only to a full moon. Personally I salute the moon whenever I see her and find that works best for me, although there *is* something about a full moon that is quite wonderful. You will probably feel highly self- conscious at first but persevere because it really does get easier.

Sometimes we notice that certain moon phases seem to have special significance for us. We may notice that certain events seem to always happen at the same stage in the moon phase. If that happens to you write it down in your notebook, it will become an important magical resource in the years to come.

If that doesn't happen to you, however, don't despair. Most people are just aware of a great power up there in the heavens, smiling down on us, like a kind mother. By doing a spell and focussing on the moon we're no longer relying solely upon our own power, but harnessing all the extra lunar energy present at that time. The best way to do this is to experiment regularly, remembering that what works for one person may not work for another.

One of the best and simplest things you can try is to get outside at night and shut the door of the house behind you if you can because this represents a symbolic break with your normal world. It need only take a few minutes and you can always say you need to take the rubbish out or call the cat or check whether the gate is closed. Obviously there *are* going to be times when the best you can manage is to look at the moon through a window. This is fine if all else fails, although some traditions suggest it's unlucky to look at a new moon through glass. In the beginning at least, do try and get outside sometimes, even for a few minutes because then there are no barriers between you and the moon. There is nothing quite like looking up at the moon on a dark night with the wind in your hair.

The first time I ever tried this, I chose fairly new, crescent shaped moon, and bowed to her nine times. (I chose nine because it is a magical number, along with three and seven. You will notice these numbers keep cropping up in folklore and even though you may not understand the exact reasoning behind it, you can make use of the idea for your own intentions.) First I bowed three times from the waist and said simply 'Greetings Moon.' Then I placed my palms together and opened them, keeping the palms upwards, bowing my head and repeating the words. I did this a further three times.

For the final three salutations I kept my gaze on the moon and extended my arms towards her, above my head in supplication. Each time my breathing was a long soft sigh, with the words spoken right at the end when I was almost out of breath. Some people prefer to speak as they exhale; some speak first and *then* exhale. It's largely a matter of personal preference. Try all three then decide which works best for you but do try and include gestures, even if it makes you feel a bit ridiculous. Gestures are a very important and ancient part of magic.

You may feel all this makes you feel like a small child. Don't worry – it's meant to! It's very important to recapture this childlike feeling – we certainly shouldn't believe that magic makes us more important or significant than anyone else. An inflated ego has no part to play in magic of any kind. It's one thing to feel happy, quite another to feel inordinately superior to everyone else.

The best types of magic *should* make us feel like a child again, imparting that special sense of wonder where everything in our world seems sparkling and mysterious. False magic – and there's a lot of it about – tends to make us feel bigger and more powerful than everything and everyone else. There's the catch. It's the difference between learning to harness and work with the moon's energies, and believing that you are going to actually command the moon (or earth, stars, wind, sea, whatever) to do your bidding. One way is the path to better magic; the other way is the path to madness and disillusionment.

It should go without saying that we should never mock or act discourteously towards the moon or any other powers we invoke. Of course, sometimes we may feel clumsy, self conscious, or lacking in grace but we must never be intentionally disrespectful. Now some people may feel this is taking things a bit far. After all, they argue, the moon is only a piece of rock.

But actually it's much than that. Our ancestors studied her, some drew and painted her, others wrote songs and poems about her, even prayed to her. They empowered her just as she empowered them. Not only does the moon have her own intrinsic power, she also has the benefit of imagery, thought and magic through the millennia. And it is the power *behind* all that imagery that gives our magic its extra force. Showing respect never diminishes us, but discourtesy and bad manners do.

How should we address the moon? Many titles have been bestowed upon her down the years, including: Goddess of the Otherworld; Goddess of the Underworld; Mistress of Birth, Life and Death; Mistress of the Earth; Queen of the Seasons; Goddess of the Sky and Goddess of Creation and Destruction. These are all quite grand, although if you addressed her as Lady Moon or even Mrs Moon, provided it was said with love, it would be just as good.

Knowing how to strip a ritual down to basics can be very useful when you have neither the money nor the privacy to do the things you would like. Often I have had to simply stand on the back doorstep, look up at the moon and whisper, 'Greetings Moon.' And the funny thing is that, more often than not, she whispers, 'Greetings, Tylluan, back to me.'

You can't fault that sort of magic, can you? Just say whatever feels right to you. It's what's in our hearts that really matters.

Chapter Eleven

Putting it all into practice...

At this point, it's time we looked at practical ways of using the skills you've learned so far. Unlike a book of spells, which offers specific spells for various situations, Magic on the Breath is a magical technique that is always with you. When confronted with a problem you simply adapt the tried and trusted techniques you've learned, rather than hunting for a 'correct' spell. What we need to do therefore is to incorporate magic into our lives, to invite it inside like an honoured guest. Once there it will repay your hospitality a thousand times, but you have to find a way to attract it to you first.

Start by examining yourself and your life to see if there are ways you can improve it magically. Done properly, magic can build character like nothing else I know! Often all that's needed is a good dose of common sense, but sometimes a magical approach may suggest a common sense solution. If you haven't performed a single spell yet and can't think what to do, then start with getting rid of negativity. You'd be surprised just how much of it there is in our lives and once you learn to deal with it you'll find your life changes very much for the better. It's time now to build on the exercises we outlined earlier in this book and discover how to incorporate them in our everyday life.

The four most common areas of negativity are probably:
- Family and friends
- Colleagues at work
- Neighbours
- Ourselves

All and any of these groups have the ability to make our lives hell. Some do it unintentionally, some accidentally, while others positively relish it. Perhaps the most difficult source of negativity to deal with is one's self, because we, more than anyone else, know exactly where to put the proverbial knife in and when to turn it. Family and friends come a close second, for very much the same reason.

For example, supposing you have a rather difficult teenage son. He spends all day and half the night at his computer, and has lost interest in school even though important exams are looming. This has caused endless arguments within the home, as he pushes at the boundaries of what you're happy to allow him to do. Minor matters suddenly become major bones of contention. Taking turns with washing up, keeping his room clean, not keeping the household awake into the small hours of the morning while he plays computer games, suddenly everything he does annoys you, and everything you say annoys him. When you remonstrate with him, he tells you he will move in with his friends where he can do what he likes. Your home, once relatively peaceful, suddenly feels like a battleground.

Obviously a large part of the solution here is going to be practical. Many teenagers go through this awkward phase and come out the other side as pleasant, well-rounded human beings. Some however never seem to grow up properly. So what do you do, short of letting him off the washing up and buying ear plugs to ensure you get a good night's sleep?

Well, obviously, there's no harm in telling your son that while he's living with you, he has to obey some house rules, and if one of those is that the computer goes off at a certain time, he has to lump it or like it. Remind him that everyone has to live with house rules. Only hermits are exempt. They can do what they like, grow their hair to their waists and wash once every ten years. The rest of us have to muddle along together – and that's what the house rules are for, so that everyone gets a fair share of privilege *and* responsibility.

As for moving in with a bunch of like-minded mates to avoid any house rules, if he does that he will probably learn the hard way that although it may be fun for a month, eventually what you get is a sort of anarchy. This in turn imposes all sorts of arbitrary house rules on everyone because while one person does what he likes the others have to accommodate him.

For example, if one person wants to play music all night, the others have to listen to it, like it or not. If one person determines never to do the washing up, someone else eventually will have to do it for him. Anarchy may be fun for a few weeks, or a couple of months, but eventually house rules come to seem like a good idea. They may even eventually work out a few house rules for themselves just to make life bearable (although he will probably never admit this to you!)

So far, this is all practical advice, equally applicable to the magically minded and the terminally sceptical. But how can we incorporate magic into this? Firstly I would suggest you carry out a thorough psychic cleansing of your home and particularly his room or areas of the house he frequents. You can begin - when he isn't around - with the sweeping exercise from Chapter Three, and when he *is* around just concentrate on your breathing. Think of it as blowing away a cloud of smoke – a stream of breath will help break this up and disperse it.

Other things you can use are candles and joss sticks – but you must light them. I met someone once who insisted that candles were no use at all; it was only later she admitted that she never actually lit her candles and liked to keep them in their cellophane wrappers! Obviously candles and joss stick need a certain amount of care since they can be fire hazards but they can be good at helping to cleanse an area. The candle flame brings light and illumination to dark situations, while incense breaks up the atmosphere and carries your intention into those hard-to-reach corners.

I find the best method is to light your candle or incense where they are needed and simply say what you want them to do. The words you use should be simple and to the point, 'Please break up the negativity in this area,' is just as good as a long, complex spell, and probably a lot less likely to be misinterpreted. You would be surprised how many people write spells that manage to say the *opposite* of what they mean! .

When using a candle to banish negativity, try and let it burn right down if possible. Sometimes you cannot do this, particularly if you are trying to keep what you are doing hidden from others in the same household, and for this exercise I find blowing the flame out is a good way of ending each session. Now I know that purists will disagree, arguing that must *never* blow out a candle flame. They believe the flame must always be snuffed out with a candle-snuffer, or pinched out with the fingers. However, since we have been working with our breath as an intrinsic part of our magic, blowing out the flame can be turned into a powerful part of the whole cleansing process. Rules are not set in stone, they can often be adapted provided you understand why and how to do it.

Salt is excellent for magical cleansing – which includes breaking up negativity - since it reduces harmful positive ions in the atmosphere. Interestingly, electrical appliances (such as computers, hi-fi systems etc.) create loads of these positive ions, so your teenage son spends hours at the computer or listening to music, he is not doing his mental or emotional state any favours.

Of course, you need to be sensible here - electrical equipment is sensitive and you cannot go washing it with salt water or throwing table salt around the room. You could however put a dish of salt crystals on the windowsill while he is out and remove them when he is due to return. Empower the salt first with a warm breath and tell it what you need it to do.

If he rarely leaves his room, put the dish of salt on other windowsills around the house. Change the salt often and either bury or burn the old stuff with a small ritual thanking it for its hard work and telling it to return to the earth (or sea, if you prefer to cast it into running water instead.) You could even dissolve it in water and sprinkle it on the ground. Use a strong exhaled breath as you finish this ritual so that the negativity absorbed in the salt does not return to you.

Negativity normally doesn't disappear in a single cleansing. It can take a great deal of effort. By the time most people realise there's a problem the negativity from your son's anger and resentment has clustered into a heavy, overpowering atmosphere (and you thought it was just his dirty socks, didn't you?) Until this is broken up you will never be able to move forward. And this of course is part of the problem, his own negativity is sticking to him like glue, he has created a thought form which is constantly feeding off him, and it becomes a vicious cycle of cause and effect.

Even when there's no cause for him to be angry, his own negativity keeps nagging at him that he *should* be. It's the psychic equivalent of him going round with a big black rain cloud stuck to his head. His anger and resentment create negativity which in turn creates yet more anger and resentment. Although cleansing your son's room has to be your main concern, don't neglect other rooms too. In particular you should attend to your own bedroom, since some of his negativity will seep into it, making it hard for you to sleep properly. It is absolutely vital that other areas of the house are kept as free as possible from his influence.

You also need to bear in mind that constant anger and conflict can harm others in the family, so make a special effort to take care of yourself psychically. I've found it helpful to do the following exercise each morning while things are difficult. It's a variation on the basic grounding exercise in this book which you can substitute if you prefer, and need only take a few minutes.

Sit on the edge of the bed and look out of the window. Imagine you are looking at a beautiful sunrise (all right, so your bedroom overlooks the local pickle factory – you'll just have to use your imagination. Take a few deep breaths to steady yourself. Now imagine you are blowing away all the unpleasantness and stress on the exhaled breaths, and drawing in strength, courage and love as you inhale. If possible you should repeat this exercise again at night. This time as you look out of the window, look up at the moon and stars. You could even step outside at some point in the evening, and salute the moon before performing the exercise.

The important thing when doing any of these exercises is to focus on your breath. Don't allow any thoughts of the problem itself to intrude because magically that will simply draw more, similar problems towards you. Concentrate *only* on dispersing negativity. The mind can only put up with so much in a day; it needs space and peace, time to recover.

Just empty your mind as much as you can, concentrating only on blowing away unpleasantness and drawing in strength and love as you breathe in. It can also help to practice careful breathing whenever your son is near. There are two good reasons for this: firstly you do not want to absorb anything negative from him, and secondly you need to try and influence him for the better.

In practice this isn't as straightforward as it sounds – your son will not be entirely negative, after all. There will only be *some* aspects of his behaviour you don't like. Also, there will be aspects of your own behaviour or habits are probably negative and could do with toning down a bit. So be aware of this when you plan your spell.

As you breathe out, imagine your breath dispersing his excess anger and challenging behaviour. Envisage your breath as a long, billowing stream. Your mouth should be held in a firm but flattened oval shape (try looking in the mirror and practising to get the shape right). Remember you are only trying to help him through a difficult stage. You don't want to even think about blowing his entire personality away, so start off in a restrained manner. You can always increase the force of the breath later if you feel the situation requires it.

Another technique is to imagine your breath changing his negative emotions into something pleasant. This is important. Never forget your own role in this. You are not an avenging angel, you are a loving parent. Some people like to envisage the teenager smiling, or becoming helpful while others find it easier to imagine something more abstract, such as their breath changing into flowers or bright colours. This is something you will need to experiment with, to find out what works best for you.

Although all these suggestions are for dealing with a teenage son, this is only an example. It can be endlessly adapted to use in other situations when you have to deal with people who are driving you up the proverbial wall. For example, if you are having problems with your boss at work you can do the same breathing exercises outlined in this chapter, this time imagining that your boss is pleased, relaxed, calmer and more pleasant than he is normally. You can certainly clear away the negativity that surrounds him. Take a look at his desk or working area. You may not be able to walk around wafting incense from a censer, but you can certainly practice your breathing exercises to clear some of the negativity away. And although you may not be able to *physically* perform the sweeping exercise, you should do it mentally even if only for a minute or two a day.

If possible you should always tackle negativity when nobody else is around. The presence of others often breaks your concentration because they interrupt, either to ask what you are doing or to bring up mundane matters. However, I know that sometimes it can be impossible to work on your own, so the best alternative is to aim for short, swift bursts of cleansing which you can fit in around other tasks. Four or five brief cleansings are better than a single long one which is interrupted.

At home, where I'm assuming you do have some privacy, you can use other methods of purification such as lighting joss sticks, incense or candles, but obviously these methods aren't suitable for most workplaces. You could however try splashing the area *lightly* with blessed water to replace the unpleasantness with something good and benign. If you are careful and use only tiny amounts (being careful to keep away from electrical or computer equipment) it's possible to do this without attracting attention. If there are plants where you work for example, you could water them with blessed water instead.

Some people worry about blessing water but it's really very simple. All you need do is add a pinch of salt to some ordinary water and place your hand just above its surface. Then you simply recite some words of blessing. These are not written in stone, and contrary to what some people may tell you, there is no special formula which guarantees success. *You* do the blessing. The power comes from within you and when you bless water your words are your own, as are your thoughts and your intentions.

All you need to say is something like, 'May this water be purified and blessed for my intentions, and may it in turn bless and purify everything it touches.' Or 'May this water bring blessings and purify everything it touches.' Some people also like to drink a small amount of the water, in which case your pinch of salt should be *extremely* small otherwise you risk projectile vomiting!

People have often asked me how soon they should expect to see a result from all this magical effort. Often there is *some* improvement within a day or two, although it can take weeks or even months before things really start to settle. One reason it can take so long is that we often don't tackle things until they're well and truly out of hand. If you act as soon as you spot a problem beginning to develop it's generally quicker and easier.

But how can we recognise negativity? One of the easiest places to start is on the road. It's quite possible to predict what some people will do once you have watched them for a few moments. Some drivers are almost always in profile, looking at their passenger as they chat; others are totally oblivious of what is going on around them and unlikely to even notice anyone before pulling out. Some are clearly late and in a hurry so they're likely to take risks; others have all the time in the world and will dawdle along at 40mph in the middle lane of the M25. It doesn't matter whether you're driving, a passenger in a car or just walking along the pavement when you try this, but you should try to minimise any distractions. So turn off the radio or CD player if possible, and certainly disengage yourself from any headphones.

When you observe how people behave you gradually learn to anticipate future behaviour. Driving is a good example because there are usually plenty drivers and pedestrians to watch. You'll soon spot which ones are exasperating, inattentive, aggressive or overly cautious. If you can spot character traits like this, then noticing negativity is the next step since all the traits I've mentioned attract their fair share of negativity.

You can use the same method in a supermarket, watching the other shoppers. Unlike people watching in traffic however, in a supermarket you will have some audio-input too, as you listen to conversations all around you. People have many different attitudes to shopping; some regard it as a social outing while others want to get it over and done with. Then there are people with more money than sense and people who count every penny. Look around you, really look, and see how many different types you can spot.

Something else you will notice in a supermarket is that negativity ends to feel quite heavy. You'll notice children become restless when they enter pockets of negativity in a supermarket. Some start crying for no apparent reason. People become short tempered and frazzled. If you look very carefully, you'll find (with practice) that negativity looks slightly darker than the surrounding area like a faint shadow.

Although books of spells don't mention this, it's a fact that a good magician observes human nature closely. We cannot distance ourselves from our own natures and unfortunately much of the time we cannot distance ourselves from other people's, either. When we perform magic we are attempting to impose our will on another person or creature. The better we understand people in general, the better we will be able to find a way to reach them.

However, there is one type of negativity that is notoriously difficult to identify – your own. Now obviously we all carry a certain amount of negativity around with us. It's impossible to remain one hundred per cent positive every hour of every day and it would be exhausting to try. Normally a little negativity doesn't do very much harm, but taken to extremes (and this can happen before we know it), it can do a great deal of damage indeed. So understanding and defeating one's own negativity isn't a luxury – in fact it's probably the single most important magical task any of us ever has to perform. Yet unless we do, we are condemned to cast spells with one hand tied behind our back.

So what is it that makes us negative? Often it can be habit. My father was fond of paraphrasing Shakespeare's *Julius Caesar*, 'A coward dies a thousand deaths, a brave man dies but once.' It's very similar with negativity. If you always look on the black side, you go through the worst scenario over and over again. If you lighten up, hope for – and expect - the best, then even if the worst happens, you only go through it *once*. Forget the accidental summoning of demons or all the other horrors people try to tell you will happen once you indulge in magic –

most of the really harmful magic is performed unknowingly in everyday life. When we say things like 'I hope I can,' or 'I think I might' we are admitting negativity into our lives because we've admitted the possibility of defeat at the outset. Worse still are phrases like 'That sort of thing always happens to me...' or 'Just my luck...'

Remember that with magic we are attempting to change the course of probability in our favour. How can we hope to do this if we don't believe: (a) that it is possible and (b) that we are capable of doing it? We must have a quiet confidence in our ability, our right to perform this magic and its eventual outcome. Although we should let go of a spell once we have cast it (otherwise our thoughts are forever pulling it back) we should also always acknowledge having cast it the spell's performance *once it has come to pass*. This gets us into the habit of accepting responsibility for any psychic fall-out. So when you have done a spell, and obtained your intention you should always mentally tell yourself 'I did such-and-such.' It should be second nature to you.

And if, unfortunately, the outcome is what you *asked* for, but not what you intended or hoped, you must acknowledge and accept your part in that, too. I don't mean you should go around beating yourself over the head for every imagined problem in the world. It's unlikely you have caused war, famine or other types of mayhem. But if you've cast a spell that hasn't gone quite as expected and has unintentionally caused some harm, you should at least admit it to yourself. You should also do your very best to repair any damage you've caused. Your magic worked but not in the way you intended.

Better luck next time.

Chapter Twelve

Some more practical uses plus Psychic Self Defence...

B ack in Chapter Three, we looked at the problem of a neighbour's dog straying into our garden. On a bigger scale, most conflicts we face in life are a variation of this – someone, somewhere is straying into our territory. What should we do about it? Often we're told to simply have a quiet word with the offending party. Unfortunately it's easier said than done and many a 'quiet word' has turned into a full scale screaming match – or worse. Another popular alternative, doing nothing while inwardly seething, offers only a quick route to stress and misery.

If we use the problem of the neighbour's dog in our garden as an example, we can devise methods that will work in other situations where someone is invading our private space and refuses to back off. Many people are quite surprised to learn that all you need is a handful of basic techniques that can be endlessly adapted and applied to other situations. Believe me, it's better to have a few easy to use methods that will work for you, than hundreds of ready-made spells that you've never tried.

If we look again at the example of the dog in the garden, we have a couple of possible options. These can all be used to make a template that we can then further adapt as necessary in future. Basically we need to find a way to send our thoughts to the dog telling him to leave the garden. Just telling him isn't enough however, we need to persuade the dog that leaving is a good idea. So the thought has to somehow be implanted into his doggy brain.

This isn't as ridiculous as it sounds. Some dogs are extremely intelligent, brighter than their owners in fact which can make them frustrated and unhappy. Of course initially at least we don't know whether we're dealing with a canine Einstein or Dopey. You might think that any dog who wanders into the neighbour's garden is probably none too bright. However he might just be lonely. And some people definitely seem to attract needy animals. You may just be one of them.

What we need here is a basic 'drive back' spell. You are going to use magic carried on the breath to drive him back to his own garden. For this you must keep your instructions clear and simple. Say exactly what you mean. You could try something like, 'You do not want to come in here today, you want to stay in your own garden. Stay in your own garden....' This will work much better than ranting 'That wretched dog is in my garden again! Why don't the owners mend the fence? Why don't they keep it in their garden etc.,' because this sort of thinking is too negative. Magic works best with positive thinking, the simpler the better. Just tell the dog to return to his own garden.

Make sure you alternate your instructions with an exhaled breath through slightly pursed lips. You need to put some – but not too much - force behind your intention. It's better to begin gently and increase the force of your breath gradually. This basic approach can be endlessly adapted to deal with difficult family members, work colleagues etc. but remember you only want to move them out of your personal space, not blow them away altogether!

A spell to drive something back can also be adapted to encourage someone to 'move aside.' This is useful to remove obstacles from your path, although I've known this type of magic also be used to persuade annoying or erratic drivers to pull in or turn off onto another road. The spell works by literally 'willing' them to make a turn while your breath supports the intentions. You project the idea into their head that they want to go somewhere else or need to pull in and make a phone call. Don't forget to keep your own mind on the road ahead if you happen to be driving as well. Some people use the same technique in supermarket checkout queues!

All this raises the question whether this type of magic is ethical. Obviously it interferes with free will. But then so does most magic. And so does virtually every law or social convention one can think of. For example, if I drive on the left hand side of the road, I'm forcing the driver coming towards me to drive on *his* left in order to avoid a collision. Free will is one of those attractive concepts that rarely work as intended in reality. However, interfering with free will is one thing, deliberately causing harm is quite another. The misuse of magic has unpleasant consequences all round – but that can also be said of most things. Driving too close to the car in front, intimidating other drivers, these are all behaviour that most of us would like to avoid. All this spell does is to try and persuade someone who is bothering us to pull over or turn off.

Driving back spells are also useful in psychic self defence. You can use the same sort of techniques to drive back evil influences, or even harmful spells although your breathing will require slightly more force behind it. As with all things you should experiment until you find what suits you. The one thing psychic self defence requires more than any other type of magic is a calm self confidence. This is not to be confused with arrogance, for that can lead us astray all too quickly. What you need is the quiet self confidence that allows the spell to be all it can.

A half hearted approach to magic rarely works. What we need is what I call the 'Toothpaste Attitude.' When you go to clean your teeth you don't say to yourself 'I hope I can clean my teeth today.' You just go to the bathroom and get on with it. This is because you know exactly what to do, and how to do it. Now, supposing you drop your toothpaste into the sink – would you panic? Of course not – you'd just squeeze some more from the tube. What if your toothbrush snapped? You'd buy another.

It's the same with psychic self defence. Just because we don't solve the problem immediately doesn't mean that we can't solve it. It just means we haven't solved it yet. Unfortunately, when we encounter problems with psychic self defence our first reaction is to often to throw up our hands and despair. Like many things in life: It Won't Work If You Don't Do It. If you give up – you'll fail.

It pays therefore to become proficient at projecting your intentions elsewhere before turning your attention to people. I've found that plants make good subjects for this type of work. Take two seeds and plant them in separate pots. Care for both equally, but talk to one of the seeds, urging it to grow bigger, faster than the other. (You will have to move it away from the other pot while you do this.) Many people find that the seed they ignore takes longer to germinate and turns into an altogether weedier plant. But this is something you have to try for yourself!

Another method is to try and project your intention onto traffic lights, willing them to stay green while you drive through. I have known people who rarely get stopped by a red light even in town centres. Of course, it goes without saying that you do not try and 'jump the lights' or drive fast and furiously to get through. Quite apart from the fact that it is dangerous and likely to cause an accident, it completely misses the point of the exercise. What you are trying to do is *make the light remain green for you*. How to do it? Well, the simplest way is simply to say 'Stay green, stay green' as you approach the light. Remember that 'Don't turn red' won't work because it is a negative command.

Some people can cause ordinary street lamps to go out (and occasionally also to make unlit lamps go on). This fascinating phenomenon is known as SLI (street lamp interference) and can also affect other electrical appliances including watches. No-one is exactly sure how it works. Some people do it involuntarily; others notice it happens more often when they are stressed.

Of course street lights do sometimes malfunction, but SLIders have been reported putting out an entire row of lights as they walk past, or putting out the same light (which never malfunctions otherwise) on a regular basis. We still don't know exactly why this happens only to some people, but there are many things we don't yet understand. The more you look in this world, the more you will find that puzzles you. Only someone with blinkers on would seriously claim there are no mysteries.

If you feel you might be under psychic attack, try and work out where it could be coming from. Usually it will be from one of the following:

- People with a lot of spite or anger (probably the most common)

- People with a great deal of occult knowledge (probably the most rare.)
- Places which have absorbed unpleasant or malevolent energies.
- Yourself

In spite of the stories you may have heard, witch-wars and all-out magical battles are not at all common. Most occultists have better things to do with their time and energies. And sometimes people are so flowing over with spite and jealousy that they accidentally launch a psychic attack.

Attacking oneself may sound ridiculous, but it's an increasingly common form of psychic aggression, and probably one of the hardest to recognise. I would suggest that, having established you really are under psychic attack, if you still cannot identify the assailant then you should assume it is a self attack and embark on a thorough programme of cleansing and clearing negativity.

There are three main methods of dealing with psychic attacks using Magic on the Breath. Firstly you should cleanse and disperse any negativity, then perform a driving back spell and finally you will need to build yourself some psychic armour. The first two build upon the idea of a strong, exhaled breath. The third is slightly different and involves visualising one protective piece of armour and one offensive piece. For example, your defensive piece could be a shield and your offensive piece could be sword, axe or dagger, basically anything that will cut.

At this point I should point out that there will always be people who disagree with using psychic weapons, arguing that they are a form of attack in themselves. Personally I believe we're entitled to fight back when attacked, whether this happens in the real world or on the psychic planes. If someone tries to hurt us, we naturally struggle against them. If our assailant uses a weapon we're justified in picking up whatever is to hand to defend ourselves. Much depends upon the situation. People comply when threatened to avoid being physically harmed. Once they *are* harmed however, they have little left to lose.

Psychic weapons are used for repelling attacks that will not respond to our unarmed responses i.e. cleansing and clearing negativity.

Before we look at the methods for dealing with psychic attacks, we need to look at the most common forms of psychic attack. There are many misconceptions about what a psychic attack actually is. People often claim that if you feel you are under psychic attack then it's probably true. Not so. Although you may well be picking up on something, it's all too easy to become paranoid.

Conversely, being blissfully unaware of a potential attack is no protection either. Although thinking only good things will hopefully attract more of the same to you on the basis of like attracting like, a determined psychic attacker really won't care whether your mind is full of sunshine and daffodils.

Sensing that something is wrong may be part of our psychic early warning system, but to be certain you should notice whether other things are present too. These include noisy psychic phenomena, a sense of dread often combined with heavy pressure on the chest especially on waking, unexplained cuts and bruises or violent, distressing nightmares. You may also notice noises that seem to come from nowhere, especially the sound of bells, and foul smells (excrement and rotting flesh are the most common). Obviously you should investigate thoroughly to see whether there is a natural explanation for any of these.

Not all psychic manifestations, even scary ones, are actual psychic attacks. There are all sorts of entities out there and some show more interest in us than others. Unfortunately it's a vicious circle where like attracts like. So if you become hysterical at the mere suggestion of occult malevolence you will attract all sorts of mischievous energies in your direction, which will make you even more hysterical and so on. Most things can be dealt with using the exercises in this book for dispersing negativity. It also helps if you can remain level-headed and calm since this will stop feeding the mischief.

Almost all psychic attacks home in on some weakness in the subject's psyche, so your personal state of mind will influence how much damage is caused. Just as being frightened attracts fear, so laughter will repel it. Here I mean a really good belly laugh, not a snide little snigger at someone else's misfortune. Although it may be the last thing you feel like doing, laughing is one of the best ways of fending off a psychic attack. Laughter is such a positive feeling it becomes a type of psychic armour and denies your attacker a chance to get a foothold in your psyche.

You can use any of the exercises already given in this book for dispersing negativity, directing your intention to the problem at hand. As you exhale using a strong, cool breath, you need to concentrate on dispersing the negativity around you and not just negativity in general. You should also practise breathing out deeply through the mouth, feeling your breath deep in your diaphragm. To empty your lungs fully it often helps to cough at the end of each exhaled breath.

Each time you breathe out, concentrate on willing the hex/psychic attack to depart. Some people like to return them to the sender; others feel this is a form of psychic attack in itself. As with many aspects of performing magic, this is a matter of personal choice.

Many hexes are created unintentionally by people with too much time and too little control over their own thoughts. Although the hex itself may manifest just like a deliberate psychic attack, there was never the same deliberate intention to cause harm. Such attacks may be better if you simply disperse them, visualising the hex disintegrating into dust and sweeping it right out of your home or personal space where it can do no more harm. Concentrate on phrases such as 'Hex – leave me. Leave those I love. I return you to dust, be harmless.'

You can also instruct, 'I make my body and spirit clean.' This is particularly good for repairing your aura, especially if you physically wash yourself at the same time, because it links a physical action with a magical intention. The one strengthens the other. Do *not* say 'I will not hex myself.' It will not work because it's a negative command. Stick to positive statements. I would recommend performing these exercises at least twice a day, morning and night. You will probably need to continue for a week after you last experience any phenomena just to be sure. After that, just do it once a day preferably at night, because this is when most problems seem to happen.

There are times however, when all the cleansing in the world isn't enough, and this is when we finally pick up our weapons and fight back. Some people equate this with mounting a psychic attack of our own, but in cases where our psychic space has been invaded and our lives are being made a misery, we have the right to block what they are doing.

As you will see, the methods of using psychic weapons are purely defensive, nothing more. You create them using Magic on the Breath and the power of your own intention. What you think, you create. It's basically a type of thought form that only you can use and activate. Although you cannot use psychic weapons to deal with a self-attack, they are invaluable for dealing with attacks from third parties.

Start by imagining what sort of weapon you'd like. Sometimes it helps to borrow a book from the library on a place or period that interests you - an eastern scimitar is quite different from a Roman sword or a pirate's cutlass. Or design your own sci-fi weapon from scratch if you prefer.

Remember though that visualising something isn't just about knowing what it looks like. Choosing a psychic emerald or ruby for the sword pommel is nowhere near as important as the weapon's size, shape, weight, and how you handle it etc. Whatever you visualise must be easy to use, just like a real weapon.

My own favourite psychic weapon was an enormous broadsword that needed two hands to wield. It was wonderful for dealing with a particularly unpleasant series of psychic attacks back when I was young. Its only drawback was that I couldn't manage a shield as well as the sword and of course for some defence work shields are vital. Eventually, when the main threat for which I had created it had passed, I created another, smaller sword plus a shield.

Whatever weapon you choose, remember that you will need to visualise it quickly, so you should practise this often until it becomes second nature, especially since some psychic attacks occur with little warning. One of the most effective methods is to name your weapon so that when you need it you can simply call out its name and it will appear in your hand.

A well created psychic sword rarely needs to be used. The threat alone will send virtually all attacks heading for cover – provided of course that you look as though you know how to use it. This is important. If you stand there with your head hanging down, self conscious and uncomfortable you will not convince anyone about your intentions. You will simply look like someone who has just picked up a sword that happens to be lying around.

Instead, stand with feet apart, your sword raised, ready to strike. Exhale several times with strong short breaths, and stand your ground. Remember that the victims of most psychic attacks never arm themselves with so much as a lucky charm, and most psychic attackers are bullies who will not attack if they suspect they will come off worst.

With a psychic shield the technique is to block anything that comes your way, and again it is essential that you look as though you know how to use it. Although ranting and constant criticism are not true psychic attacks, they can cause a great deal of very similar damage. Luckily they respond very well to the magical techniques we have looked at in this chapter.

It is very important however to disregard the *substance* of the criticism as much as possible. Even if you cannot ignore the fact that you're being criticised, you don't have to justify yourself to your accuser. It's vital to avoid putting any more negativity or anger into the situation. Anger feeds off itself – the more there is, the more powerful it becomes. It gathers momentum so quickly like a snowball rolling down a hill that the situation can get out of hand without warning. Just visualise raising the shield at the moment the other person starts to speak, and let their unpleasant comments bounce off harmlessly.

Some people also like to imagine the negativity striking sparks off the shield – if you feel it helps then by all means use this imagery. Your breathing for shield work is to calm and steady yourself. Sometimes, especially in the early days, you may need to keep the shield in place for some time. This is easier if you aim for a long exhaled breath through slightly pursed lips. Keep as relaxed as possible so that you don't tire easily.

Repeat this for as often as necessary and don't lower your shield until the other person has left you alone. No matter how persistent your attacker appears to be, take heart from the fact that you will rarely if ever, come up against a trained occultist. Most psychic attacks are built upon a combination of spite, resentment and a person who has far too much time on his hands.

Most psychic attackers try to dominate you in some way, often trying to get inside your aura so that you feel their presence like a dark shadow before you even know they are around. You may notice they seem to stare unnervingly at you whenever they speak. Although it's natural to look at your companion when having a conversation, if you feel physically weakened afterwards it suggests you've been under some sort of attack. In situations like this a psychic shield is essential and you should not be afraid to use it whenever such people are around. They soon pick up on the fact that they cannot get through to you and back off. Even so, remain alert whenever they're around.

Other attackers seem to drain the life force out of you. These are sometimes called psychic vampires. I always think this term is rather misleading, since these people don't actually cause you to wake up covered in bite marks or scratches. If you do wake up with scratches etc., they are usually caused by full-scale psychic attacks, either from someone who knows exactly what they're doing or from entities with vampiric tendencies who have attached themselves to certain places.

Years ago I briefly moved into a very unpleasant house and began waking each morning covered in what looked like mosquito bites although it was the middle of winter. Disinfecting the place from top to bottom made no difference; the problem only stopped following prolonged psychic self-defence and energetic cleansing. Even when everything had settled down I was still glad to move away.

The most worrying thing about psychic vampires is that they feed off your energy. Just as houses with strong psychic phenomena often have massive electricity bills because the psychic activity is 'feeding' off the power supply, so some people 'feed' off other's energy. Usually they have to be physically nearby for this to work, although I have known one or two psychic vampires who do their work over the telephone. Psychic attacks do seem to be getting more hi-tech all the time!

Vampirism isn't always deliberate or even done consciously; some people don't realise they're subconsciously topping up their own energy by siphoning off other people's. The end result is the same for the victim however: debilitating, often unexplained illness.

Whether or not some is attacking you by trying to drain, dominate or scare you half to death, they all set up some kind of link to their victims. If they see us often, then the link will be some sort of psychic cord that connects them to us. If they don't have physical contact with us very often then they usually try and leave something – often as a gift – that has some sort of hex embedded in it.

To find a psychic cord, look at how the hexer behaves when they are with you. Usually they either fix you with a stare or shut their eyes. There is a good reason for this: when you engage with other people you set up a link from their Third Eye (which is in the centre of the forehead, just above the bridge of the nose) to ours. Psychics often describe it as a very thin reddish line, a bit like a length of thread. Its purpose is to enable free exchange of ideas and thoughts and normally this can be helpful. However when used in a psychic attack, this line can become thick and tough, and all the thought flows just *one way* making it easy for an attacker to dominate the victim. Alternatively, a psychic 'vampire' can download all your energy and life force via the thickened cord, rather like a computer cable.

So our first task must be to prevent any cord from thickening and sever the connection. This is where our psychic armour comes in handy. A psychic shield can prevent the attacker from setting up any red cord whatsoever while a psychic sword can cut a pre-existing connection. Remember though that attackers will try anything to distract you and make you drop your guard, so don't let your mind wander while you do this. Stay focussed. To use the shield you just raise it to cover your face, while keeping up a steady relaxed breathing. To cut a pre-existing cord, you have to visualise cutting the connection with your sword or dagger. Think of it as putting down the receiver on an abusive phone call. You are not severing your connection with the rest of humanity, just that one person.

Some people like to create a special psychic weapon especially for cutting through cords, especially if they're on the receiving end of a great deal of psychic aggression. These weapons can include golden scissors, axes and even lawnmowers! It doesn't matter as long as you feel comfortable with them.

Sometimes we can underestimate the nature of a cord and then it can be difficult to cut so don't just visualise what it looks like, try to imagine what it *feels* like too – is it thick, brittle, slippery or like wire? Never be afraid to allow your weapon to adapt. If you choose to cut the cord with a pair of psychic nail scissors and it turns out to be as hard as iron, you just have to tell yourself that your scissors are as strong as any wire cutters and will slice through it like butter. The real power is in the mind and will, not the weapon.

Whatever weapon you decide to use, take one good breath before you act, aim for the middle of the cord and exhale strongly until it is severed. It can also help to mentally say, 'Enough. I am breaking this tie between us once and for all.' Then breathe several more times, again very strongly, in order to blow the cord away and prevent the ends from reattaching themselves.

If you prefer to have something to say, then still keeping the same breathing pattern, try :

> *I have the strength to cut this cord,*
> *And henceforth you shall be ignored.*

Usually the effects of your actions are immediate, especially if the cord has only recently been set up. However sometimes you find that your attacker will increase the frequency and intensity of their efforts. If that happens, simply keep blocking them with your shield and cutting through any red cords they set up. Be persistent and don't give up. There are no half measures in dealing with psychic attacks and most will stop completely within a week or two. Once any connection between you and your attacker has been severed, remember to keep up your shield to prevent new attachments being made. Usually the situation will settle down given time, although personally I would never relax my guard when dealing with these individuals, even at a much later date.

Sometimes hexes deliberately target those we love instead of us. At other times a poorly directed psychic attack can ricochet off the intended victim and hurt others (including pets) in the vicinity. It's therefore important to magically cleanse your living and working spaces while you are under psychic attack. All you need is your breath and your intention to cleanse.

However at times like this I recognise that we sometimes feel the need to 'do something' because it makes us feel empowered. The important thing is to keep concentrating on the exhaled breath as you work. There are a variety of techniques that you can add to Magic on the Breath, such as strewing salt, dipping a brush in blessed water and spattering it around, burning incense and lighting candles. Beware though that salt and blessed water can damage furnishings and electrical equipment, while incense burned on charcoal blocks will play havoc with your smoke alarms. Candles should always be used with care.

One of the easiest methods of cleansing is to ring a bell in each area you want to cleanse and rely upon the vibrations of pure sound to support your breath and your intention. Obviously your intention has to come first: what do you want? Exactly? Don't fudge this, even with cleansing otherwise you may get rid of things you may wish you'd kept. Think it through and keep it simple, especially when you're just setting out. For example, it's no use laying a trail of salt around your boundaries while thinking about what you want for tea! Having something to say can be help focus our intention and you might want to try any or all of the following:

- *Protect this home and all who dwell therein.*
- *Let no evil enter this place*
- *May no harm come to the people who live here.*
- *Protect this home, protect those I love.*
- *Go back, you cannot enter here.*

As always, stick to simple, straightforward commands in your magic because they are precise and not open to misinterpretation.

Sometimes people complain that this doesn't *feel* as though they are casting a spell; they convince themselves that spells must always rhyme. Of course the big pitfall with rhyming spells is that unless you keep a very tight leash on them it's all too easy to get carried away with the poetry and lose the original meaning. So here I'd like to show you here how I wrote a rhyming spell to drive back harm. Originally I started off with:

> *Evil thoughts and evil deeds,*
> *I pluck you out like errant weeds.*

I thought the second line sounded a bit vague (if not downright incomprehensible) so I changed it to '*Go back, you shall not sow your seeds.*' While this looked all right on paper, that line can be a bit of a tongue twister. For line three I thought I would reverse the first line. However, '*Evil deeds and evil thoughts*' gave me a few problems when it came to finding a rhyme for line four. So I changed it to '*evil deeds and thought be gone.*' After that I decided to make the spell turned back the attack to its sender. Thus the finished spell was:

Evil thoughts and evil deeds,
Go back, you cannot not sow your seeds.
Evil deeds and thoughts be gone,
I send you back, where you belong.

Whenever we send a hex back, chances are it will almost certainly rebound on its creator. There are those who feel this is akin to mounting a psychic attack of our own, but I disagree. We have not gone looking for trouble. On the contrary, it has been sent to seek us out. All we have done is the equivalent of saying, 'No thank you, you can keep it,' and sending it back. There is nothing wrong with this. Surely it's better to send the hex straight back to the wretched person who created it rather than allowing it to rattle around and hurt some innocent third party? In my opinion and experience sending the hex back to its creator is probably the best – if not the only - place for it.

If you are convinced you're under attack but have little physical contact with the person you suspect is the culprit, you should check whether they have recently given you anything unusual. Many hexes require the victim to have willingly accepted an item from their attacker, especially pictures concealing magical symbols whether or not the original image has been tampered with although obviously if an image *has* been tampered with we have to assume that the hex is deliberate. Some hexers are very creative in this department using fur, grasses, leather, horn or anything else that has once had life while others prefer to work with crystals and stones. Once I even came across a hexer who conveyed her attack via a souvenir tea towel given as a gift!

So, let's suppose you have discovered something in your home that you believe is being used to convey a psychic attack. What do you do first? Your first reaction is probably to throw it away, but it's better if you can neutralise the hex first otherwise it will (a) continue to bother you or (b) possibly go and attach itself to someone else. Begin by taking a few steadying breaths to ground yourself then breathe on the item using a strong exhaled breath between firmly pursed lips. All the while, visualise the hex disintegrating. You have to be as firm about this as you possibly can, show the hex that you mean business!

Personally I usually burn objects that have been used for hexing, then sprinkle the ashes with salt and finally cast them into running water. This isn't always possible, and if everything else fails simply bury the object in plenty of salt (cheap table salt will do.) At every stage of the disposal of the item, remember to focus on your breathing.

Concentrate on blowing away any harm that was attached to the object, so that it crumbles to nothing. Since dust has a tendency to attract negativity anyway, make sure you perform some thorough psychic cleansing around your home or office afterwards.

Sometimes a hex will attach itself to something valuable, such as a piece of jewellery. This is because the attacker knows you're less likely to dispose of it even if you suspect it is carrying a hex. If this happens, and you really cannot bear to part from it, then you will have to thoroughly cleanse it on a daily basis if necessary. Magical cleansing alone can do the trick on this type of item, but much depends upon the skill of the hexer and also on your own determination. This is no time for half measures. Do the cleansing rituals forcefully and regularly. Be prepared to continue for at least a week after you last notice any disturbances.

Interestingly, the same principle applies to things we buy second hand, and especially to items we find. Often we have no way of knowing whether these were ever meant to be discovered. Sometimes potentially harmful things are hidden in the hope that no-one will ever handle them again; sometimes objects are left where others can pick them up as a means of conveying a spell to a third party. This method was often used in wart charming.

Finally, when dealing with a psychic attack you should remain calm. Magic on the Breath is particularly helpful in this respect since concentrating on your breathing helps suppress anxiety and fear. It very easy to over react and become paranoid, imagining that psychic attackers lurk around every corner. They don't.

But if you do encounter any problems now you'll know exactly what to do.

Chapter Thirteen
Amulets and Talismans

J ust as you cannot power a car from a gas oven, nor switch on a household light with a steam engine, so you have to find the right 'type' of magic for each spell. Magic on the Breath is particularly versatile in this respect, because it links our intention (i.e. the purpose of our spell) with that most basic physical function: breathing.

However, no matter what method we use in our magic, it also makes sense to do whatever we can physically to assist our magic. It's no good casting a love spell yet taking no *practical* steps to make someone notice you. Likewise it's no use casting a spell to procure a new job and not bothering to send off your application form!

A book of ready written spells – no matter how big it is - can only do so much. It cannot accommodate every situation. Also it tends to make us lazy, because instead of working on the spell ourselves and building up our power as we do so, we sit there looking at the index instead. Far too many people simply day dream about casting a spell but never get around to doing something to make it happen. This is probably the single biggest obstacle to successful magic. If you want something then you must make the effort to achieve it. You will not win the lottery if you cannot be bothered to buy a ticket and check the numbers. Likewise your spells will never work if they remain firmly stuck between in the pages of a book.

Rather than make the effort themselves however, some people will ask a friend to cast a spell for them. You've probably noticed this already if you've ever mentioned that you're interested in magic and it's very easy to become snowed under with such requests. It's not that people lack the knowledge to cast a spell - after all, they could learn if they really wanted to. Usually they are just too lazy to do anything to help themselves. It's *so* much easier to get someone else to do all the hard work!

Occasionally they're also cowardly. I was once asked – by someone I barely knew – if I would hex her ex-boyfriend. I had no intention of doing this, but admit the request intrigued me. When I asked why she chose me, she replied, 'Well, I don't want any fallout from the spell to harm me.' I suppose that merits ten out of ten for honesty and one out of ten for integrity!

The worst thing about 'spell-beggers' is that so often their requests are unrealistic or unreasonable. Some will try and make you feel it's your duty to help them, accusing you of pursuing only personal gain if you refuse. Yet refuse you must – or at least strictly ration the help you give - unless you want to end up drained of all energy. Nobody has the right to make you feel like that, and you are doing yourself no favours at all if you allow them to do so.

Of course, magic isn't just about doing spells. You can, for example empower objects to protect yourself. Welcome to the magical world of amulets and talismans. The two are often confused but are actually quite different so we will deal with that first. One definition is that a talisman is designed to bring its owner good luck or to assist her in some magical function whereas an amulet simply protects against magical and psychic attacks, disease, and general bad luck or harm. At home I have a row of very large, bright coloured glass balls, red, gold, silver, blue and green, like giant Christmas tree decorations. These are Victorian Witch Balls, designed to catch the Evil Eye, and avert any harm intended to the occupants of the house. Because they are protective, these could be classed as amulets. The 'lucky charm' carried by gamblers, however, is usually considered a talisman.

Another definition is that an amulet is something that has to be worn, carried or possessed, engraved on stone, metal or some other hard and permanent material. Once created, it offers long lasting protection. A talisman however can be written on paper, parchment or even leather, created under the most favourable astrological conditions and only intended to benefit a specific event for a single individual or group. Both amulets and talismans are extremely ancient traditions that you can adapt or copy to suit your own magical intentions.

Sometimes talismans and amulets are not created at all, but are found. For example, some people believe finding bent pins or nails brings luck; the Italian tenor Pavarotti was rumoured to search for lost nails before each performance. Unusual objects are also often regarded as 'lucky.'

For example, stones containing natural holes were used to protect against witchcraft and were either carried in the pocket or worn threaded on a piece of string or leather. They were even attached to the key of a stable door, to protect the horses within from being elf shot or bewitched. You could adapt this by attaching a holed stone to your keys to protect your house or car.

Horseshoes are traditionally regarded as lucky, and if you look at them with the curve at the base they resemble the horns of Cernunnos, the ancient horned god of the Celts. Being made of iron they are also associated with blacksmithing deities, such as Wayland Smith, Vulcan, or Hephaistos. Iron is also a powerful amulet against elves, and fairies, and perhaps the modern equivalent might be to protect against alien abduction!

Because they look like the crescent moon, horseshoes are also useful if you want to work with one of the many moon goddesses. Traditionally they are simply hung up, usually near a doorway or gate, but you could empower them further using your breath and your intention just as you do for any other amulet. Remember that if you buy or obtain someone else's good luck charm you should cleanse it thoroughly. One man's luck may be another's misfortune!

As with all things magical, things you make yourself are more effective because they are tailor-made for a given situation and because of the effort you put into creating them. What matters is the effort not the object. You must imbue your talisman/amulet with your intention, literally breathing into it so that it absorbs your magical will. Remember though that talismans bringing luck in love may be powerless when it comes to finding you a parking space! Also, your talisman/amulet doesn't need to be elaborate. Often the plainest looking charms are the most potent.

When you're ready to start, think carefully about what you're asking for. In my spell-writing workshops, one of the most common problems is in actually making the first move. Few things are more daunting than staring at a blank sheet of paper. The important thing however is to make a start. Think of magic as a building with many doors, and all you have to do is find one that will open for you.

Resist the urge to panic. It happens to all of us at one time or another. Write your ideas down, leave them for a day or so and then return to them - often when we see them again we realise they weren't so good after all! If you still can't think of anything, try another angle.

For example, what is your favourite colour? Supposing it's red. Now think about why you like it, and what it reminds you of. For example, possibly the colour reminds you of fire, and warmth on cold winter days. In that case use either red ink or red paper for any intention that involves making you feel warm or cosy. So *for you*, red might be ideal for love spells, or anything connected with the home. Someone else might associate red with blood and use it in healing work instead.

You can also trigger your imagination by using the four elements, earth, fire, air and water. For example, certain colours might suggest one or more of the elements. A very rough guide might be as follows:

- Red, pink, orange, peach, gold - fire
- Bright blue, grey, silver - water
- Green, gold, brown, black - earth
- Pale Blue, pale grey, silver, white - air

In Chapter Seven we looked at using the elements to strengthen our spell work. Water, for example, is associated with the emotions, healing and can attract psychic influences. So you could use any of these suggestions and choose a colour associated with water, such as bright blue. You could then create your charm in blue ink, or silver ink on blue paper. This would be quite suitable for any talisman or amulet involved in healing, divination, or even dispelling emotional baggage.

Earth colours could be suitable for protecting our home, families, or job. The element of air is closely involved with intellect and thought, and colours associated with it could be used for any talisman/amulet connected with examinations, studying or problem solving. Fire is closely associated with the intuition and imagination, so can strengthen a talisman intended to promote following our dreams, identifying and protecting us from false friends. Of course, these are only suggestions. Use whatever feels right to you: it is your talisman, not mine.

Although some people recommend using Rune symbols or zodiac signs I would not recommend these unless you are *already* comfortable working with them. If you don't have enough knowledge to fully understand an established symbol then leave it alone until you do. Otherwise you could, for example, use the zodiacal sign for Scorpio to represent a particular person born under that sign but accidentally end up representing *someone else* who happens to share that birth sign instead. Once you understand established symbols then by all means use them as seems right to you.

If you need to create a talisman or amulet in a hurry but don't have time to learn about symbols such as runes etc., first, then it's better to create your own. At least then it will be personal to you. A stick figure with meaning is far more powerful than a realistic portrait without magical intent. Spend some time – when you're not actually creating a talisman/amulet – creating your own magical shorthand of symbols and images. It will stand you in good stead in the future and the effort you put in down the years will make such symbols remarkably powerful in your magical work.

Remember to enjoy the magical process, not suffer it. A certain amount of light-hearted fun is not only permissible, but necessary because it helps you relax. Tension and anxiety will tie the best of spells into knots and render them ineffective. One way to loosen up while creating symbols for your talisman/amulet is the childhood game of 'taking the dog for a walk.' All you need for this is a pen or pencil and pieces of paper ranging from quite small (about the size of a postcard) to very large (poster sized – off cuts of wallpaper will do.)

Beginning with the smallest sized sheet first, just doodle, thinking of the talisman you want to make but *not* trying to draw anything in particular, just allowing the pen to roam in an uninterrupted line. Round and round the paper – it will look like a mess, but that's part of the fun – doubling back on itself, twisting, turning, filling up every part with sweeping rhythmic lines.

Remember to keep thinking about your 'intention' i.e. what you hope to achieve.   Your breath should be relaxed and steady, pausing sometimes to breathe directly onto the paper to fix your intention. The best type of breath for this is a warm breath, the sort you would use to make a mirror mist up.

Then do the same thing again, using the next size of paper, until finally you are working on the biggest sheet. This will be the hardest because there is so much more space to cover, and you might find a felt pen or marker will be easier to use than a biro or pencil. But the process is the same: a long, twisting, rambling, unbroken line covering the entire sheet. When you worked with the smallest sheet you probably used only your fingers and possibly your wrist to draw. With the largest sheet you will have to use your whole arm and even your shoulder. Remember though, you're not trying to produce a work of art, but to create intense, spontaneous symbolism.   Experiment with different pens, pencils and even charcoal.   Paint isn't suitable though because you would need to keep breaking off and dipping your brush in more colour.

When you have finished, examine what you drew.   You'll probably notice that the doodles on the largest sheet will be more fluid and flowing. Look for a small part of the design that 'speaks' to you and which you can reproduce in your talisman.   Don't worry that your squiggles appear totally unconnected with your magical intention – as long as you were relaxed and concentrated on the matter in hand as you drew, your design *will* have absorbed your intention.

Whatever material you decide to use, (e.g. paper, parchment, leather etc.), you can probably place symbols on both the front and reverse, but remember you only have *one* intention. So if your intention is, 'I want to make John Doe fall in love with me,' you must find at least two ways of doing this and four if you fold the paper in half. Having used the 'taking the dog for a walk' method for side one, you could write your name and his on the second side. This is pretty basic, and you might want to ensure that your names were properly linked. For example, if your name was Jane Smith, you might try writing the first letter of your name, then the first of his, then the second letter of your name and the second of his and so on, like this:

JJAONHENSDMOTEH

Alternatively, see whether it's possible to portray a name in picture form. For example, apart from obviously names such as Carpenter, Baker, Butcher etc., there are names like Cooper (a barrel maker) and Fletcher (an arrow maker). If you do use this method however, you must remain very focused on the actual person represented in the picture.

Some people swear by magical alphabets, such as the Theban Alphabet. While this can impart a sense of 'otherness' to your work, separating it from the everyday world, it's not essential if you've worked on your symbolism properly and focussed your intention into your breath. Magical alphabets have no power of their own; it is what *you* bring to them that makes them special. You certainly shouldn't expect them to be a substitute for the real work of magic: the intention and the breath.

One simple and popular method of creating a talisman/amulet is to fold your paper and cut out a circle, being careful to leave a 'hinge' so they can be opened out, rather like a birthday card. It doesn't have to be a circle; you could use a star shape or triangle if you felt it was more suitable. One advantage of a folded shape is that you have four surfaces to write on instead of only two. This gives you plenty of choice, but remember that each surface needs to be cleansed before working and then empowered once the piece is finished. You do this using the power of your breath and by concentrating upon your intention, i.e. cleansing or empowering.

Even if you decide to only work on two of the four available surfaces, the blank sides must still be fixed in this way since they are an intrinsic part of the charm. It can be any size, although I always prefer something small enough to carry in the pocket. There are no hard and fast rules, but don't add decoration for decoration's sake. Every mark should have a purpose.

What should you write on your talisman/amulet? The simple answer is whatever seems appropriate. First and foremost, don't forget to clearly identify the subject of your work. It's all too easy to get carried away and forget the basic purpose! That said, don't be tempted to write reams either. A simple, meaningful symbol can speak volumes provided you have first distilled all your intention, all your power, into a single sign.

Don't be afraid to try – far more spells are ruined through timidity than recklessness. Magic is a hands-on operation. It won't work if you don't do it. If you're frightened you'll make a mistake then start off with simple, straightforward intentions, such as protecting objects or healing. Once you become more confident you will be able to tackle most things that come your way.

The glyphs or symbols on your talisman are best written in something permanent, such as Indian or acrylic ink, and may be either left as an outline or coloured in. Obviously you should avoid making it too cluttered. Some people like to perfume their ink with a drop of an appropriate essential oil – just *one* tiny drop though, or the ink will be difficult to work with.

If you are using paper make sure it has been sized so that the ink can't 'bleed' into it. If you can get hold of a piece of real parchment this would make a longer lasting talisman, but be careful since much of what is sold in art shops is actually paper with the *appearance* of parchment rather than the real thing. Of course you can still use it, but again test first for 'bleeding.'

You could also use cloth - preferably linen or pure cotton - and either embroider the symbols or paint them on with fabric marker. However one drawback of cloth is that it won't allow you to work on both sides because the stitches or marker will show through. This means you will end up with some *reversed* symbols which could have the effect of negating the intention altogether! Never begrudge time spent checking these things and experimenting; it too, is all part of the magic.

Sometimes people express surprise that I still take quite a long time to create my talismans and amulets. They imagine that because I've been doing this for so long that I will just be able to pluck the right charm out of thin air and all will be well. But magic doesn't work like that. If something is worth achieving, it's worth making the effort. Go to your local library and research plants, stones, deities etc., which might have particular associations with the type of charm you want to create. Possibly you already feel drawn to certain things and identify with them. Sometimes these are self evident – my own name, Tylluan, is the Welsh word for owl so many of my talismans incorporate an owl shape in them somewhere!

In the early days at least, try and get a feel for magic first before you try tackling more complex methods. Beginners who start with complicated invocations to a host of entities are making life hard for themselves. If you later want to use ceremonial or ritual magic, all well and good, but these are difficult for beginners to master. Magic on the Breath may look simple but done properly it's extremely powerful. For many years now it's the only method I ever use.

Important: *Don't be afraid to change and adapt until you have worked out precisely what you want to achieve. It is all this mental energy and soul searching that will go into the finished product. This is why home-made talismans and amulets can be so very powerful. You cannot just buy them and expect them to work. If you do buy one, you should still make the effort to work with it in order to build up its power.*

Almost any natural material can be used to make a talisman. I've known people swear by lucky pebbles and shells they find while walking on the beach. Others engrave their symbols onto metal, which you can sometimes obtain from a good craft shop. I have nothing against man made materials; a talisman intended to influence modern technology might work better if it is made of plastic or silicone.

Another example would be using a pebble or stone for a talisman designed to help you find the house of your dreams, or an amulet to protect your home. Metal might be the obvious choice for any charm connected with cars or machinery. Paper would be good for amulets or talismans connected with studying, letters and knowledge while fabric might be most suitable for anything connected with the home, our appearance and everyday living. It's all a matter of finding something appropriate for your intended purpose.

You may be advised to choose a metal with a suitable planetary connection, for example, gold for the sun, lead for Saturn, silver or tin for Jupiter, iron for Mars, tin for Mercury, copper for Venus and silver for the Moon. However, few of us can find such materials, let alone afford some of them. When in doubt therefore, stick with paper; it's the easiest material to get hold of, comes in a wide variety of textures and colours and doesn't require any special skills or equipment to write on. You can always use metallic coloured inks to establish your planetary connection and what you lack in precious metals can easily be made up with good breathing and the power of your will.

Whatever material you eventually choose to work with, remember to purify or cleanse it first. Some believe the best way to do this is to put crystals on it, pass it through incense, or even leave it out beneath a full moon. Others may prefer to use 'cleansing spells' to rid the paper of any negative energies before (and sometimes after) you apply the symbols. However, with Magic on the Breath, the means of cleansing and empowering lies *within you*. You don't need any tools unless you really want to use them. Even then, they should always be subordinate to the power of your will and your breath.

In order to cleanse say, a paper talisman, you just cut out the shape. Then hold it on the palm of your hand so that its flat surface is parallel to the ground, just below the level of your mouth. Breathe gently (so you don't blow it away!) aiming for a 'cool' breath. If you experiment first, you'll find that if you blow quite firmly with your lips *slightly* pursed, your breath feels cool, whereas if you blow softly, with your jaw slack, making a soft 'hah' sound your breath feels warm.

Important: *A cool breath has a clearing or cleansing action, a warm breath can empower.*

You don't actually have to say anything when you cleanse your talisman but if you do then make it simple and to the point. 'Be cleansed and receive my marks of power' is just as good as any long incantation. Or simply visualise blowing negativity away as though it was some sort of psychic confetti! Don't worry about the talisman's intention at this stage, concentrate only on cleansing it. The best time for this is before you *first* start working on it and ideally you should complete drawing the symbols at a single sitting. If you leave it only part done then it could attract other energies in the interval before you start working on it again. Repeated cleansings are not the answer either, since they will just undo all the power you've built up so far.

Some people like to prepare a stack of 'blanks' so that they always have one ready. However you rarely need a talisman or amulet in such a tearing hurry that you don't have time to start from scratch. Also you will imbue your magical work with far more power if you keep every intention completely separate. Even the work of cutting out is an added opportunity for empowerment, so if you are using blanks you will miss out on this.

Just as there is no single right way of cleansing, so there is no single correct method of empowering. Just remember that all you're trying to do is to infuse your talisman/amulet with the power of your intention. It's all about what's in your mind, not what colour candle you've chosen. Unlike cleansing which should be done at the start, empowering is done when everything is completed. Pick a time when you know you won't be disturbed and lay the talisman out so you can see it clearly.

Sit comfortably and do some deep breathing to ground yourself. Now, using a 'warm' breath, breathe just firmly enough over the talisman/ amulet to make the paper flutter. You might have to move it slightly closer towards you although remember you don't want to blow it away! If you have used metal, leather or card however, you should use a 'warm' breathe instead, breathing as firmly as possible while thinking of your magical intention. You will probably need several of these breaths - some people like to do three, seven or nine since these are regarded as magical numbers, but you can use any number that has meaning for you. For example, a person's age or the number of years they have been married.

Of course, sometimes it can be hard to concentrate on your intention, especially when you're nearing the end. All the hard work has been done and you're naturally excited that your work is coming to fruition. However you must make the effort to avoid letting your mind wander. Many a potentially powerful talisman has been wrecked at the final stage when its maker starts thinking of doing the washing up or cleaning the windows instead of keeping focussed on the job in hand!

Chapter Fourteen

Glamour Magic and Invisibility Spells...

Glamour Magic is probably one of the most secretive types of spell-work you will ever encounter. People might tell their friends or families if they're having Botox or surgery, but it's rare they'll ever admit to standing in front of a mirror and doing Glamour Magic. It smacks too much of the wicked stepmother in Snow White, looking in the mirror and asking, 'Who is the fairest of them all?' And yet, done properly, this sort of magic does work. I have known people look ten to twenty years younger using it. It's not just women who do glamour spells, either. For men they also offer the promise of youthfulness without the embarrassment or expense of surgery, injections or creams.

But Glamour Magic isn't just about transforming your appearance or changing your eye or hair colour. Frankly if that's all you want you should go and buy coloured contact lenses and some hair dye! Glamour spells are much more subtle (and powerful) than that. Done well, they not only roll back a couple of years but also allow you to look like the sort of person you really want to be, along with getting rid of the wrinkles and crows' feet.

What you're really doing is not enhancing your appearance but magically empowering *yourself*. So please forget everything you may have heard about gazing soulfully into mirrors of a specific shade of pink and demanding to be beautiful. It's not like that at all.

The old saying that beauty is in the eye of the beholder is perfectly true. What one person holds beautiful, another may find plain or even repulsive. Beauty is nothing if beheld by someone who is incapable of appreciating it. But Glamour Magic Glamour is so *much* more powerful than mere beauty. It can cast its spell upon both its creator and all who behold him (or her.) The word 'glamour' actually derives from the same source as 'grammar' suggesting that both were originally associated with learning.

Glamour magic is extremely subtle in the way it works, but no less powerful for that. It teaches you, first and foremost, to like yourself. This is particularly important nowadays when so many people find it impossible to look in the mirror without flinching. Indeed, some parts of the media actively encourage this, because it's a powerful way of making people fearful and insecure.

Listen to groups of people (especially women) talking and time and again you will hear them discussing the latest diet fad. Or Botox. Or plastic surgery. Or all three. All that talk nowadays about wanting to be a size zero; you could be forgiven for thinking that people won't be satisfied until they've made themselves invisible!

And of course this contributes to the problems people have with their own self image. Self loathing has become the norm. Years ago when religion had more influence on daily life, people were taught to view themselves as miserable sinners. Nowadays the media encourages us to view ourselves as fat, plain, or in dire need of cosmetic enhancement. Really, we should be able to look at ourselves and think, 'Not bad, considering I've had a couple of children and I never have enough money to buy smart clothes,' or 'Yes, never mind my figure, I've got great hair/skin/teeth/a lovely smile.'

Instead women and men are being browbeaten into believing they must fit into some pre-ordained mould that takes no cognisance of the reality of their lives. The result is that they are never happy, because they are never allowed to *learn to like themselves*. Why else would such profitable industries have arisen around the wild promises of the latest diets or the surgeon's knife?

Whether we know it or not, we regularly perform magic in everyday life. Usually however, it's only of the negative variety. If you doubt this, then consider: How many times do you hear people putting themselves down when they talk? In the end this almost always becomes a self- fulfilling prophecy which is still a form of magic. If you look at yourself in the mirror and convince yourself you are ugly, this will ultimately reflect not only how you see yourself, but how you allow others to see you. This is because the ugly image you insist of believing is of you, affects how you present yourself, talk about yourself, and yes, the way you expect others to treat you. In effect, *you will become ugly*. Or fat. Or whatever your particular hang-up happens to be.

On the other hand, if you look at yourself in a kindly light, you are giving yourself a chance to become the person you want to be. It *is* possible to achieve much of this simply by positive thinking – but where the magic takes over is in turning what you initially 'feel' about yourself into reality.

Years ago, people believed the camera could not lie. We now know that it can – spectacularly. Yet many of us still convince ourselves that our mirrors cannot lie and unquestioningly accept what they tell us. The truth is that mirrors can, and often do lie. Indeed, some of them are very wayward creatures.

How often do we read in newspapers and magazines about slim – even thin - people who somehow convince themselves they are enormous? Or clearly beautiful people who believe they look like trolls? Every time they look in the mirror all they see is a hideously distorted image looking back at them. This in turn influences their view of themselves, and how they feel others must see them. It doesn't matter that family and friends tell them they've got wonderful figures and beautiful faces, they would much rather believe the mirror.

Glamour spells are the reverse of this. With this type of magic, no matter what your defects, every time you look in the mirror you see yourself as attractive, youthful and pleasant (assuming that's what you want to see!). This in turn influences how you view yourself, and how you feel others must see you. Given time - since this type of magic offers no quick fixes - others will indeed come to see you quite differently, and in accordance with the way you see yourself.

So how is it done? In principle, Glamour Magic is no different from any other type of magic you have done so far since it involves driving back – in this case driving back the signs of ageing - and creating a thought form, both of which you have already encountered. However, of all the types of magic you are likely to practise, Glamour Magic is probably the most demanding. You need to do it regularly (every day if possible) for as long as you want the effects to last. You cannot do a 'bit' of Glamour Magic – it's an ongoing process that offers amazing results *if you stick at it*. If you're not prepared to do this you might as well go and buy the hair dye and coloured contact lenses.

Glamour Magic works much better if you use the same mirror for your work. When you look in the mirror a small part of yourself seems to rub off on it. Not all mirrors have the same character. Some are spiteful and cruel. Stand in front of one of these every day and you will indeed convince yourself that you look like a rhinoceros.

This seems to be a two-way process. In the same way that constant negative thought will build you a loathsome thought form, so constantly denigrating yourself in front of a mirror will turn your looking glass into a cruel, hyper-critical tormentor. And some mirrors seem to be particularly attuned to criticism. It *is* possible to make a mirror more sympathetic but this requires time, skill and effort.

Mirrors create illusions of space and light, but they have their own powers too. When I was young, adults would often warn children against looking in them for too long. It was believed that if you gazed at your reflection more than three times a day you would be sure to see the devil, horns and all, standing behind you! Whenever someone died, all the mirrors in the house were traditionally turned to the wall or covered with a dark cloth. This was in order to set their spirit free, since it was believed that the dead person's soul could become trapped in a looking glass and remain earthbound. And of course even nowadays, mirrors are still used for scrying, deflecting hexes and summoning spirits.

One reason why mirrors fascinate us so much is because they can show us ourselves. Imagine a world without them, where you only saw everything going on around you, but were never able to see how you fitted in. A mirror can show you things that nothing else can. A photograph will show a static image, a camcorder will show you an image taken moments or even years previously. Only a mirror shows you the here and now, and in some miraculous way manages to reverse the image! It shows you the ravages of time and sorrow, or the blessings of love and happiness. Make no mistake; mirrors are extremely potent magical tools.

The earliest mirrors often came with their own cover, not just to protect the polished surface (in those days made of metal rather than glass) but also to lock in the magic that might otherwise ensnare the unwary in his reflection. To the ancient mindset, this was a very real danger. In classical legend, Narcissus pined away and died because he became enchanted with his reflection in a pool and abandoned real life.

The old superstition that breaking a mirror brought seven years' bad luck could well have been based upon the length of time it can take to build up a real relationship with your mirror. If your special mirror was broken then you had to start afresh and begin 'breaking in' a new one.

Before you begin to work some Glamour Magic you should spend some time sorting through your mirrors, the larger the better. In my experience you cannot do successful Glamour magic using the mirror in your powder compact or even a hand held glass. One family member assures me it *is* possible, although the mirror in question is an antique silver one that had been locked in a drawer for some years.

Having seen it, I am sure it has been benignly enchanted as some point, although I still feel this mirror is the exception rather than the rule. A wall mirror is ideal, as long as it is free from cracks and blotches. You may have to experiment quite a bit before you find something you like. When you start looking you will be surprised how much variety there is, not just in the frame but also in the quality of the glass itself.

Although when we say something is a 'mirror' image we mean that it's identical, the truth is that mirrors can vary quite a bit. Some have a slightly blue tone, so you always seem to view yourself in harsh daylight; others are very slightly golden, which is generally more flattering. Some make you look larger, others smaller. Take no notice of the frame; it's the glass which matters in this sort of magic.

Ideally you will start with a mirror which feels 'friendly' and is large enough to reflect at least your head and shoulders. A good quality looking glass is 'close' to you. You can check this for yourself by placing the tip of your index finger against the glass. In a good quality mirror your finger should 'touch' its reflection. Poorer quality mirrors will have a distinct gap so that the reflection appears further away.

Obviously it's best to avoid a glass that is blotched or cracked. Old mirrors in particular often suffer when the silvering on its reverse side begins peeling off or flaking away. An antique mirror, no matter how lovely, is not necessarily the best looking glass for Glamour Magic. If your mirror has bevelled edges try and keep your reflection away from them since they distort your image and you don't want to end up looking like an escapee from the Hall of Mirrors!

The main reason for using a large mirror is that the spell will work on all those areas of your body that are reflected in the mirror. In my own experience I think standing between two and three feet away from the glass is the ideal distance. However, if that means that all you can see is part of your face, it stands to reason that the results of your magic will be a bit uneven. I have a lovely old Victorian mirror on my dressing table, showing my reflection from my waist upwards – the result is that the lower half of my body is rather creaky and definitely not as good as the top half since it has been 'left behind' in the magical working! Normally you can only work with one mirror at a time so choose carefully.

Even using a full length mirror is not without its drawbacks. Although it gives all-over coverage you may have to stand too far away to concentrate on your face. Of course this may not matter if you feel that a wrinkle or two is a small price to pay for sorting out your figure! The choice is yours but remember there will always be something you cannot cover such as your back or feet. In magic, just as in other aspects of life, you are never going to find perfection. Just deal with it.

Cleansing is essential before you start, and you should allow plenty of time for this. Even if your mirror is brand new you shouldn't omit this stage, since even in a shop other people may have been looking in it and it may have absorbed their energies. Using a 'cool' breath (see Chapter 13 for this), mentally blow away any negativity. With a large mirror this can take quite a bit of time and effort but it's well worth it. You should also make sure you do the same for the area around and even, if necessary, behind the mirror.

When you first begin working with Glamour magic it can help a great deal if you dispel any negativity in your home, and particularly in the room where you keep your mirror. You should also make sure you ground yourself before working with the mirror. This is the equivalent of having a psychic shower. You feel cleansed and energised which is always a good state to be in when attempting any magical work.

After cleansing is complete, polish the glass as you would normally, while still concentrating on your exhaled breaths in order to prevent any negativity from seeping back. Next take a new duster and breathe on the glass, using a 'warm' breath. If you are going to make this mirror your cherished friend you'll need to imbue it with as much of your own self as possible. This may even involve talking to your reflection, affirming that you are going to learn to like each other, and become the sort of person you dream of being.

Now stop – what sort of person *do* you dream of being? If all you want is to look like a Barbie doll or the latest celebrity then Glamour magic will disappoint you. Beauty is much, much more than skin deep. You have to subject yourself to some pretty intense introspection to find out who you are really capable of becoming. But anything worth achieving is going to require effort, and wouldn't it be worth the effort if you could finally look in the mirror and see (and like) the 'real you'? You can't expect others to see the light that shines within if you keep the curtains closed!

Now obviously I appreciate this can be difficult, especially if you've grown used to the idea of looking in the mirror and wincing at what you see. If this is how you feel, begin by changing the lighting in some way. For example, if you draw the curtains a little you'll notice your reflection becomes hazier and softer. Or you could try placing a small lamp nearby, and adjusting it so that the shadows and highlights are more flattering. This isn't cheating, just a way of getting to know yourself – and your mirror. As soon as you feel more comfortable, then you can return to more normal lighting although some people always like the odd candlelit session in front of their mirror.

One thing you must not do is to tense up. View it all as fun. Get a torch, turn off the lights and look at your reflection as you change the position of the torch beam. From the side, from above, even pointing upwards towards your chin. See yourself by candlelight provided you make sure you don't burn yourself or set fire to anything! With make-up, without, fully clothed and naked, let your mirror see you are you are. Yes, some views will be amazing, others may be scary but everything will be *you*. And much of it will be a version of yourself that you may never have noticed before. The mirror can offer many images, not just one. It can flatter, cajole, criticise and encourage, it can distort and enhance your image. But at the end of the day, you are – you must be – the one in charge. You alone can direct and control what it will do.

One of the most important things we can do in magic is to open our minds to certain possibilities. A closed mind is like a closed book. You will never know what's inside unless you open it! I can't give you an *exact* recipe that will make you look ten years younger because what works for me will not necessarily work for you.

Remember that you are always in charge of your mirror. They can be very wayward things, so never attempt Glamour Magic if you are feeling tired or unwell. You need to be fully in control for this, but also playful and light hearted because your mirror will feed off your anxiety and play on your fears given half a chance – at least until it recognises you're in charge. In Glamour Magic your mirror is your tool, and you must be its master. However, you should also treat it kindly, since a resentful mirror is a foul thing. Make a point of always smiling to your reflection and greeting it. Remember how pleased it makes you feel when someone tells you how well you're looking and make a point of paying yourself a compliment in the mirror, every single day.

So far you may think that all we are doing is simply empowering ourselves, and learning to ignore our bad points. This of course is true, but it's not the whole story. You are learning to control your mirror, how it conveys information to you, and this is part of the magical process. Someone once tried to tell me, in all seriousness, that a certain potion was essential for all glamour magic, plus I would need a dozen rose pink candles for the spell. This is nonsense. There is no quick fix magical solution to the way we look. Over a period of time, however, transformation *can* be achieved provided we make a continued effort. Nobody else can do it for us.

Another bit of advice you can safely ignore is to gaze deeply - or even soulfully - into the mirror. Frankly the depth of your gaze makes little difference and is quite liable to give you a headache if you overdo it! Be practical. Begin by looking for your good points. This is not the time for false modesty - *everybody* has good points. They may be obvious, like beautiful hair, or more subtle, such as lovely fingernails. List them to yourself, notice how good they look. All the time you do this, you breathe out using a warm breath to empower the mirror to notice these too. It doesn't have to take long, just a few moments each day, and particularly when you are getting ready to go out somewhere.

After a while you'll notice that you feel more comfortable seeing your own reflection. If your mirror feels uncooperative, praise it for its colour, its shape – anything positive you can think of. It's rare indeed to find a completely negative mirror. That said I've come across one or two especially in pub toilets, who react to your reflection though they would like to rip out your windpipe and replace it with a length of garden hose! I suspect they have absorbed far too much negative energy over the years and you should certainly never attempt to work with such a mirror at home.

A common criticism of Glamour Magic is that it's simply a form of positive thinking. This is only partly true, and certainly not the whole picture. That would be like saying that driving a car is all about the steering wheel! Mirrors are very powerful tools, and can exert their influence *whether you use them intentionally or not*. Some are certainly more kindly than others, and some are downright cruel. Some encourage a pleasant self image, others virtually scream at you. If you stand in front of any mirror being self critical all you are going to do is teach it how to criticise and ridicule you. Stand in front of one that already has a good dose of spite in its makeup and you will soon feel you ought to go around with a sack over your head.

When you want to exert your will upon the mirror you must lean forward and breathe on it mentally stating your intention as you do so - just as you would for any other intention. You must be precise about this. For example, you might think 'I want to be slimmer' would be a good intention. But would it be good if you suffered an illness that made you lose weight? Also you should avoid giving negative or ambiguous directions. 'I am going to lose some weight from my upper arms' is better than 'I wish my arms weren't so fat.'

As with other types of magic, you should help your intentions along with some active, physical effort. It would be no good doing magic in order to pass an important exam and yet refuse to do any revision. Yet some people will insist that magic somehow *ought* to be able to overcome this, and that giving your magic a helping hand is somehow cheating.

This is absolute nonsense. Everything we try to do, whether magical or not, benefits from a bit of help whenever possible. So if you're embarking on a course of Glamour Magic, remember to pay *physical* attention to your appearance too. Little and often is the best approach to this sort of magic. Several very brief sessions in a day are much better than a single long one.

Centuries ago, Alexander the Great was confronted by something called the Gordian Knot. Legend said that whoever could untie the knot would rule the whole of Asia Minor, but it soon became clear that it was an impossible task. Finally, exasperated, Alexander said, 'What does it matter how I lose it?' and simply cut through it with his sword. There is nothing particularly virtuous about taking the long way round something rather than heading for the nearest shortcut. Magic is exactly the same. If it's possible to give it a helping hand then you should do so. Successful magic relies heavily on common sense.

Don't be tempted to rub the glass (or yourself) with anything that pretends to be a special Glamour magic potion. They don't work and usually all you end up with is an oily mirror (or skin) and a streaky reflection. However you can set up an oil burner with a few drops of good quality essential oil nearby to create a pleasantly fragrant environment.

Over a period of time – and this differs from person to person – you will find that you begin to enjoy these periods in front of the mirror, a sure sign that your magic is working.

Invisibility Spells

I thought long and hard about including this section, because so many people believe it really belongs in fiction. And yet... there are cases where people manage to get past security guards and that sort of thing. A famous example concerns the psychic Wolf Messing, who was ordered by the Soviet leader, Stalin, to rob a bank using only the power his mind. Messing apparently achieved this by convincing all the security guards and bank staff that he was in fact someone else. They not only let him into the bank but also gave him the money without question. Invisibility is not simply about disappearing, it's about manipulating other people's perceptions. In effect, Messing persuaded others to misinterpret and overlook him.

While I hope you're never called upon to rob a bank, Magic on the Breath is actually very good for any type of work requiring secrecy because it can be performed without attracting attention. You should always use a cool breath to 'blow away' recognition of what surrounds us. Don't overdo it, though, because often what we need to remove is only a tiny portion of the whole.

For example, if you were trying to make a bad mark disappear from an essay, you would not be able to make it disappear completely forever, and nor should you even try. What you could do however, is to cause the mark to go unnoticed by someone else, or make it seem better than it really is. If you overdo the spell you risk making the essay itself disappear altogether. It's really just a question of getting the balance right.

Luckily – for those who wish to try this sort of magic for themselves – many human beings have a natural talent for invisibility spells. If you doubt this, ask yourself how many times you've felt 'invisible' in a group of people? How many times have you felt overlooked or undervalued? Yet you're just as real and as substantial as anyone else. We're all made of the same organic matter, we can think, we have feelings. But some of us – and I suspect they may even be in the majority – seem to go through life almost unnoticed. We're never chosen for anything, often overlooked and apparently invisible. Indeed at the time, especially in childhood and adolescence, this tends to feel like a disadvantage. But if you consider it from a different angle you'll realise that in fact, you have a natural talent for invisibility magic.

To perform invisibility magic – whether it's to make ourselves, someone else, or something else unseen to others – we need to return to that childhood state. I say childhood because we are more magically aware and powerful as children, at least until we learn – or are forced - to conform. And that of course is how we learn not to be invisible – by learning to fit in. It's important though not to return to old feelings of worthlessness or isolation because they came *after* we'd been unnoticed by others. What we need to rediscover is what rendered us invisible in the first place.

Sometimes it can help to think how others viewed us at that time. Remember that invisibility magic doesn't make us disappear; it simply changes others' perceptions of us. So think back to those times... did we perhaps try too hard to join in? Did we try to smile too often, to laugh at others' jokes, to make ourselves fit in? Sometimes we succeeded rather too well, and instead of simply fitting in with our peer group we made ourselves blend right into the background instead. Another possibility is that we consciously set ourselves apart, becoming observers rather than participants.

However we managed to achieve invisibility when we were young, we probably all used slightly different methods. This is why each of us has to experiment in order to find out what works for us now. This is not a cop out. Magic is a very personal thing. Finding a method is just the start, in order to develop the technique we have to work within the boundaries of our own character and personality. It's not difficult, but it does require practice to literally blow away what others perceive. And you can do it using the power of your mind and your breath.

Invisibility magic also requires careful examination of a situation before you begin. As an individual, you only have a limited amount of energy, so you need to decide the most efficient way of working. You rarely need to influence the perception of everyone in the area. Usually just one person will suffice, because if something gets past them, others will accept it as being authorised. If you wanted to change the perception about the mark you had for an essay, for example, then provided the first person to see it did not register that it was a poor mark, nothing would be said and there would be little or no fuss.

If you don't learn to be efficient, you will waste your power and your magic will suffer as a result. Often good spell-casters perform poorly simply because they try to do too much, or they drain themselves by performing too many spells for other people. It's not that they cannot perform magic, or that the technique doesn't work: they are simply not giving themselves a chance. It would be a bit like playing a game of football immediately before running a marathon.

When you do invisibility or any other type of magic, remember that you need to persevere. Never give up at the first hurdle. Nowadays many people seem to think that real magic is just as they see it on television – a quick flash of light or a shower of sparks and it's all taken care of. Real magic isn't like that, and never was. Even when it seems as if nothing is happening, keep trying. Perseverance and patience are both essential qualities in a good spell-caster.

Chapter Fifteen
Some final thoughts...

As I've said before, no book can give you all the spells you'll ever need. It can however give you some useful tools so you can start experimenting for yourself. The different types of magic you have learned here concentrate on a few basic practices. Dispersing negativity, creating thought forms, 'driving back spells' and self-empowerment or Glamour spells, can all be used imaginatively.

For example, don't just drive back the neighbour's dog; try using the same technique to drive back illness, or heartache or loneliness. Try driving back other bidders on E-bay! Use these ideas, stretch them to their limits, see what they will and will not help you achieve. Make notes all the time so you can refer back to them. As I've said before, magic is not just about muttering a few words and lighting the 'correct' coloured candle. You're trying to manipulate a situation to your own advantage.

I know at this point some people start to panic. The idea of manipulating anything makes them feel uneasy as though we are doing something we shouldn't. Yet we manipulate natural laws to our advantage every day. Think of it. Would you hang clothes out to dry on a rainy day? Of course not. Wet weather = wet clothes.

Would you expect to put a pound of butter into a hot oven without it melting? Again, no, because you know that butter becomes liquid at high temperatures. All the time we mentally exploit the natural laws of the world around us without a second thought. Using the magic in this book is simply extending the way we employ such laws.

Each of us has great magical potential, great stores of untapped power. It's just a question of exploring it. When we first learn to swim we are taught not to go out of our depth; swimming is fine, provided you can put your feet on the bottom. Some people remain at this stage all their lives while others go on to swim the English Channel or dive off the top board in their local pool. It's all a question of experimenting, and stopping when you feel you've tested – and reached – your limits. You don't have to be timid, but you don't have to be too reckless, either. With magic you're simply trying to recover your own sacred powers and learn to use them wisely.

Time and again I come across the idea that we must not do magic that interferes with another's free will. This assumes that all wills are not only free but also equal. Yet supposing a person's 'free will' is to run down the street attacking other people? Is that free will really sacrosanct? You see, it's all a question of quality: free will is only as good as the intention behind it. Time and again in everyday life we make decisions that interfere to a greater or lesser extent with the way another person wants to live their life. Somehow we convince ourselves that we have greater insight into their lives than they do.

How many times have you heard someone saying, 'I only want what's best for you (or him, or her, or them),' to excuse blatant meddling which many a magician would never even con-template? For example, in the 1970's a number of 'cult-busters' sprang up. Their function was to 'rescue' people who had gone to live in the communes set up by new religious movements, and to return them to their parents. This often involved what was basically kidnapping and brainwashing, although some were accused of worse.

It wasn't even as though the 'children' concerned were very young. Some were in their twenties, others in their thirties. If that wasn't interfering in another's free will then I don't know what is! Yet such actions were often excused and condoned on the grounds that the parents only wanted what was 'best' for their children, i.e. to return to the family's own religion and values.

The ideal guideline for your magical work is to consider what is acceptable in everyday life and adapt accordingly. This requires far more effort than the 'an it harm none' idea, and a readiness to make good any injury you accidentally cause. Remember there is no such thing as 'black' or 'white' magic, only good or bad intentions.

A good intention is straightforward and what I call 'true' – it's like looking down a length of wood and seeing that it's totally straight. A bad intention is not true; when we examine it we can see it's twisted and should be avoided.

However, even a good intention can sometimes become warped. This is just as true in everyday life as it is in magical practice. Love is a wonderful thing – but an embittered love is a monster shunned by everyone. Likewise there's nothing wrong with being ambitious – but once this becomes twisted you will cheerfully destroy anyone or anything that gets in your way.

Just about anything you can think of has a positive and a negative aspect. You can use medical science to find a cure for cancer, or to create biological weapons and sell them to the highest bidder. You can drive a car safely and take your grandmother to hospital, or drive like a maniac and kill another road user.

Magic *is* powerful, and all power brings its own temptations. But power, like love or ambition, is not intrinsically bad in itself and we exercise authority and control in all sorts of small ways in everyday life. If we can be trusted to do that, then we can surely be trusted to use magic sensibly and responsibly.

Likewise magic will not make you prone to hasty, ill-considered actions unless you are already prone to act in this way. If you are calm and sensible in your everyday life, there is no reason your magic should be any different. Although Magic on the Breath is a very quick and effective technique, you still need to prepare your intention properly. And it is this preparation and thought that should give us chance to cool off.

Never cast your spells in a rage. Anger is one thing, and it can be used positively in some circumstances. Rage however can distort our intention and easily hit the wrong target. Always give yourself chance to calm down before casting a spell. Often you'll end up deciding not to go ahead with it.

A good comparison is the difference between writing a letter and an email. To write a letter you have to collect paper and pen, find somewhere quiet and marshal your thoughts together before even starting to write. Then when it's written you must put a stamp on the envelope and take it to a post box. With an email you simply sit at your computer and fire off one email after another. Many a person has regretted a hasty response that might never have been written if he had given himself to simply sit down and think about it first.

It's therefore important with *all* forms of magic not to be hasty. Sometimes a mere five minutes thought is all that is required to calm us down. There are few situations indeed where we cannot spare a few moments to sensibly consider our magical options. Magic on the Breath makes use of the power that exists within all of us to harness and influence the natural laws to our advantage. As with most things, it can be used wisely, unwisely or not at all. One of the biggest risks with any type of magic is that you can become so involved with it that you cease to operate in the real world. Magic should be a means of enriching your life, not replacing it. As with all things, you should keep it in perspective. Your magic is always much better and more powerful when you keep a firm grip on reality.

As you progress you will find there are many different methods of casting spells. Don't be afraid to try them unless they contain certain aspects (such as sacrifice) that you find abhorrent. One advantage of starting off with a simple system such as Magic on the Breath is that even as you become more experienced and yes, more adventurous, you are never afraid to strip any spell down to its basics. Nobody should ever be able to brow beat you into doing something you don't like. For example, some people believe that pain is necessary (usually in the form of some sort of sacrifice) for a spell to work. You now know otherwise.

But just in case you are tempted, you should ask yourself a few questions: whose pain? Why should the pain and distress of a third person (even a willing participant) or animal aid your magic in any way? And how much pain are we talking about? Try wearing a rubber band around your wrist and pinging it hard against your skin at the moment when this supposedly 'essential' ritual should be taking place. It will certainly hurt but is unlikely to do you any harm. But it's most unlikely to enhance your spell, either. Using your breath to direct your magic may sound laughably simple, but done properly it can be as powerful as any other system - and indeed more powerful than most.

Another thing you will come across in your magical journey is the idea of magical words. Religion and the occult are full of them. Again you will need to test them for yourself. From my own experience, I have found the words 'twtch yn twtch' to be excellent for pacifying and defusing situations, and also for making restless children (and pets) go to sleep. I have no idea of their literal meaning, nor indeed whether they actually have ever *meant* anything. They look as though they could be Welsh, but I suspect they come from the early written English for the word 'touch.' So what we are *really* saying is 'touch and touch'.

Why are they magical? I don't know. But it's something I have tested and tried and found to work. Of course it can be (and is) used by non magical adepts too. The fact that it seems to have survived the strong non-Conformist background of the South Wales Valleys points to its usefulness and power. Nowadays the word 'twtch' is some sort of computer spyware, so I suppose the words would no longer appeal to modern computer-wise magicians!

You will find it is much easier to start with a simple system that works and then refine it to suit your own needs rather than starting off with a complicated system requiring tables of correspondences and endless calculations before you dare lift your wand (always supposing you can find it!) and utter a few magic words.

One of the great advantages of Magic on the Breath is that it allows you to remain inconspicuous. Nobody needs to know what you're doing. There are no incantations or gestures, and this is why I believe it remained a viable method of magic even during times of persecution. Most of the people arrested for witchcraft in Britain centuries ago had often either threatened their neighbours or drawn attention to what they were doing in some way. Yet others must have gone on practising without attracting the authorities' attention, passing their skills down from one generation to another.

It's very important to avoid drawing attention to yourself when casting your spells. Magic is a private matter not a stage show. Teaching magic skill to those who are truly interested is one thing, but people who stride down the street wearing long robes and carrying a broomstick are not proving anything to anyone.

Important: *Magic is all in the doing, not the appearance of doing.*

When I was young nobody ever admitted to doing magic, not even within the family. Magic was performed – in my family it was usually hexing – but not discussed. In fact the whole idea of witchcraft, magic and even the paranormal was simply dismissed as nonsense. At the time I thought it was strange, especially when it was obvious that *something* was going on. However that was how things were done in those days and now that I am older I can understand why. The Witchcraft Act was not repealed until the early 1950's and I suspect many people felt there was a possibility that less tolerant times could always return. Certainly we should value our privacy. Once gone, it's well nigh impossible to get it back.

This book is designed to get you started using a powerful but curiously simple magical technique. How you use it – how often, and to what purpose – is your choice. Now it's time to set out on your own journey, building on what you've learned here. You have the tools, and your will and your breath are always your own. Think of them as the raw materials. Some people will build magical palaces while others may get no further than a magical kitchen cupboard. You do what seems right and appropriate for you and take responsibility for your own actions.

Congratulations. This is the end of the book... but the beginning of what I hope will be a very long, inspiring and successful lifetime of magic!